EXMOOR W[

A Microstudy by

Noel Allen and Caroline Giddens

The Exmoor Press

Dulverton TA22 9EX

Preface

In 1988 the Exmoor Natural History Society published a comprehensive volume, entitled *The Flora and Fauna of Exmoor National Park. A Provisional Check-List,* containing 272 pages of detailed information about more than 5,000 species. This was a remarkable achievement and deservedly won a prize in the competition organised by the European Year of the Environment. The purpose of this new Microstudy is to convey, in the form of an easy-to-read narrative, the four main elements of wildlife on Exmoor contained in the Check-List: namely Mammals, Bird Life, Insects, and Plant Life. For other subjects, e.g. Fish and River Life, the reader is recommended to consult Noel Allen's Microstudy, *The Waters of Exmoor* (Exmoor Press, £1.50) or the Check-List itself.

The authors of this Microstudy were co-editors (with Heather Bristow) of the Check-List. Noel Allen is the founder and chairman of the Natural History Society, and the author of several Microstudies as well as other works. Caroline Giddens is Secretary of the Society and has herself written several books, notably *The Flowers of Exmoor* (Alcombe Books).

© Noel Allen and Caroline Giddens

First published 1989

ISBN 0 900131 60 8

All rights reserved.

Illustrations

The source of each picture is indicated on the relevant page.

Front Cover: Fox Cubs (David Doble)
Back Cover: Red Deer (David Doble)

Printed in Great Britain by Williton Printers, Somerset

Contents

Coastal Woods, Porlock Weir to the Foreland.

Mike Barbee

1 Introducing Exmoor

Exmoor is the second smallest of the ten National Parks in England and Wales, but it is unrivalled in the beauty and variety of its landscape and in its rich flora and fauna. With so much of our countryside disappearing every year beneath the concrete of new dwellings, industrial estates, roads, airports and reservoirs, the wisdom of establishing our National Parks becomes more obvious every day.

Exmoor was designated a National Park in 1954, and over the years there have been many battles to preserve the uniqueness and wildness of Exmoor from conifer plantations, ploughing of heather moorland, and draining of important wet areas. However, the fight is being won, though not without heavy casualties and the need for constant vigilance. Almost everyone now recognises the value of our open countryside and wildlife in fostering our physical and spiritual well-being, a quality of life that Exmoor with its lovely hills and valleys, rivers, woods and coast, does so much to realise.

Today, Exmoor covers 265 square miles, about two-thirds in West Somerset and the rest in North Devon. It is administered by a National Park Officer and his staff from Exmoor House, Dulverton. The Park Authority owns nearly 7,000 acres and has management agreements over a further 4,000 acres. Nearly 20,000 acres are in the care of the National Trust, and the Forestry Commission owns about 3,000 acres. The rest is either common land or privately owned. There are 40,000 acres of open moorland, equally divided between heather and grass, much of it lying between 1,000 and 1,700 feet above sea level. Woodlands total 16,500 acres, about half broad-leaved; and there are 300 miles of rivers and major waters, and 30 miles of coast extending from Minehead to Combe Martin. More than fifty villages and hamlets with a population of about 11,000 lie within the Park, mainly along the coast and in the foothills. Bridleways and footpaths total some 600 miles. This very briefly is the varied countryside where we find Exmoor's plant and wildlife described in this book.

With the future of the landscape of Exmoor now reasonably assured, backed by the watching brief of the National Park Authority, the conservation policy of the National Trust, and the regular monitoring by voluntary conservation bodies, the existing flora and fauna are in good measure safeguarded. The wild red deer, fox and badger and dozens of other creatures, the hundred or so species of nesting birds, and the vast numbers of butterflies, moths and plants, are all for us to observe and enjoy; but they are also a heritage for us to protect for future generations.

A big Exmoor stag with hind and yearling.

David Dahle

2 Mammals

Exmoor has 31 native mammals plus six introduced species. Some like the red deer, fox and hare are well known and regularly seen, but others are much less conspicuous. The badger, hedgehog and dormouse are mainly nocturnal; the mole, weasel, and stoat are by nature secretive; the otter, bank vole and water shrew are rare. All are ancient dwellers on Exmoor, each with a fascination of its own which adds much to the richness of Exmoor's wildlife.

Deer

Exmoor can boast three species of deer: red deer, with a population of c. 1200; fallow and roe deer with between 200 and 300 each. At one time sika deer were living wild along the southern border of Exmoor after escaping from Pixton Park, Dulverton, but they seem to have either died out or inter-bred with red deer. We also have had a few reports of muntjac, an unspotted brownish deer, not much larger than a big dog. Should this become established on Exmoor, it is likely to increase rapidly in woodlands and gorse brakes.

Distribution of Red Deer

Most of the wild red deer live in three main areas, with the greatest concentration (of about 30 per cent) in the northern part, mostly on National Trust land. Here are small herds harbouring in all the principal combes from Robin How to Lucott Cross and using the 900 acres of the Horner Woods as a safe refuge. The largest herds of up to 35 are likely to be seen above Langcombe, on Tarr Ball, and across Chetsford Water on Little and Great Hill. A regular herd grazes Ley Hill, and a few hinds seem to live permanently on Crawter. Herds may join up for a while especially when hunted or persistently disturbed, and we have counted groups of over 100 on these occasions. Over the past 20 years we have walked from Cloutsham Gate to Lucott Cross times without number and rarely if ever failed to see red deer. Grabbist Hill and North Hill surrounding Minehead both hold resident deer, others harbour in the coastal woods from Worthy to the Forelands, and they can often be seen on Porlock Common above Shillets and Hawkcombe woods. Red deer wander westwards into Weir Water and Weir Wood, on to Mill Hill and down into Hoscombe, Chalk Water and on into the old Royal Forest around Larkbarrow and the top of the Pinfords. Recently five stags spent the summer at the back of Badgworthy Wood feeding mainly on Brendon Common. Apart from occasional deer in Farley Woods and a few in woodland bordering the lower Heddon Valley, deer are scarce west of the Simonsbath to Lynton road. The total deer population in this northern part of Exmoor is about 400.

The second main group of red deer harbour in the valley of the river Exe from just below Warren Farm all the way down to Exebridge, and around its two main tributaries, the Quarme and the Haddeo. This is a quite thickly wooded area from Winsford onwards, and deer not easy to count, but herds of 15 to 25 are often seen feeding in clearings and in nearby fields. The probable total here is about 250.

The Barle Valley below Withypool and the Danesbrook form the third main red deer stronghold within the National Park. Again this is a well-wooded area, but we have counted 70 deer on West Anstey Common and 25 just below Withypool, and smaller groups in Bradley Woods and near Marsh Bridge. These two valleys and the wooded hill slopes probably hold some 200 deer.

In addition to these three main areas there are red deer in Stowey Woods, on Croydon and Brendon Hills, and around Heasley Mill. In fact, there is hardly a corner of Exmoor which is not visited at some time by them, and immediately south of the National Park there are several hundred deer in the Bray and Yeo valleys.

Red Deer—The Pride of Exmoor

These are the largest wild animals in Britain today, adult stags standing 45 inches at the shoulder, and hinds six inches less. They are stately in form and movement and add great beauty to the landscape. Antlers are grown only by stags and are shed in April and early May; new ones start to grow immediately. Calves are born in June, with a few in July, and are usually dropped in moorland vegetation or by a woodland edge. A single calf is normal, and twins a great rarity. For a few days it will lie quietly, well camouflaged with dappled spots on its russet coat looking like sunlight on dead bracken. Soon it is strong enough to run with its mother and to join the herd, keeping together for a year or more.

Red deer eat a wide variety of food, including young shoots of heather, whortleberry, bramble, saplings and grass. They also feed on acorns, fungi, berries, ivy, and will raid the farmer's fields for corn and root crops. They have eight biting teeth in front of the lower jaw, and none immediately above, biting against a hard gum pad. This often means that a shoot is bitten half through and then torn away, leaving a characteristic red deer trail. Footprints on the ground are called 'slots', and are a ready indication that deer are around. Hair on barbed wire, racks, or breaks in hedges and vegetation at regular crossing places are also useful signs.

Outside the autumn rut red deer normally form separate stag and hind herds, but mixed groups can often be seen throughout the year. A single big stag or a hind with her yearling are also fairly common especially in the less frequented parts of Exmoor. They are mainly silent animals, but hinds will bark at intruders especially when their young are about, or to give warning to the rest of the herd. During the rut in October and November, the belling or roaring of stags echoes across many a combe as darkness gathers. Their hearing and sight is good and the sense of smell highly developed, and it is difficult to approach them except down-wind. Red deer are healthy animals, but are getting old at twelve years, and probably few live beyond their fifteenth year. They have no predators apart from man.

Fallow Deer

These are about two-thirds the size of red deer and can be found in an area east of the A396 Dunster to Wheddon Cross road, but rarely elsewhere on Exmoor. The best places to find them are on Gallox Hill above Dunster near the two circular Iron Age forts, and in the Forestry Commission plantation on Croydon Hill. Others roam around Hart Cleave and Stowey, and eastwards on the Brendons to Monksilver. We have seen herds of up to 20 in these areas, and they are descendants of deer which escaped from Dunster Castle and Nettlecombe Court.

Most of the fallow deer on Exmoor are very dark, almost black in winter, and very few have the typical light brown coat, spotted white. Their life-cycle is much like that of the red deer; bucks dropping their palmated antlers in May, the fawns born in June and able to run with the doe within a few days. A good identification point is the long black, white-edged, tail which is constantly on the swish.

Roe Deer

This small deer, half the size of the red, was common throughout Great Britain in Norman times, then rapidly declined in England to the point of extinction. In 1800 the Earl of Dorchester released some in Dorset, and from these and other 19th century introductions, roe deer have slowly colonized much of southern England. At the same time roe deer from Scotland have spread down into northern England, and these two main groups, estimated at half-a-million, will eventually meet up in the Midlands.

A red deer calf remains hidden in the undergrowth until big enough to run with its mother.

John Keene

Roe deer live in family groups and not in herds, with the normal unit consisting of buck, doe, and twin kids of the year. They are largely woodland animals feeding on shoots, leaves, and grass. The buck carries short, straight antlers which are cast in November and re-grown during the winter. Apart from the small size the points to note are the white caudal (rump) disc, and the absence of any visible tail apart from a tuft of hair grown by the doe in winter.

Roe deer were first seen on Exmoor about fifty years ago but were rare until 1970. Since then there has been a steady increase, extending to the Brendons and down into the more secure coastal woods. We have encountered them in all the main woods from North Hill, Minehead, to the Forelands; and other sightings have been in Luccombe Plantation, Horner Woods, Hawkcombe, and the East Lyn Valley above Watersmeet.

Badger

Next to the deer, the badger is the largest wild animal living on Exmoor. Adult badgers, foxes, and otters are all about three feet long, but the average badger weighs some 25lbs., and is twice as heavy as the others. Badgers are certainly old inhabitants of Exmoor. Brockwell near Wootton Courtenay is an ancient hamlet and 'brock' still lives in the vicinity. They also appear regularly in 17th and 18th century churchwardens' accounts where one shilling was the regular local payment for killing a 'grey'.

Badgers do generally appear grey but individual body hairs are white at the base and tip, and black in the middle. The head is white with two broad black stripes running from behind the ears and down through the eyes to the pinkish snout. The short, stout legs and underparts are black, and the stubby tail whitish-grey. With long claws and strong limbs they are well equipped for digging out their burrows or 'setts' as they are called. Badgers also have powerful jaws, and trapped or injured animals must be handled with extreme caution.

There are badger setts over much of Exmoor up to the 1,000-foot contour, usually on sloping ground which is not easily flooded. We know of some with a dozen entrances and extending for 30 yards or more, which must be hundreds of years old. They show a preference for old, broad-leaved woodland and thick hedgerows with big trees, especially if there are plenty of brambles, gorse, or bracken around so that they can leave and return to the sett unseen.

Badger population on Exmoor is well up to the national average on the lower wooded and agricultural land, but there are very few on the high

11

moor. With four setts per square mile on suitable ground, there are some 500 setts in the National Park, with a total badger population of around 2,000. Badgers are frequent road casualties with peak figures in spring and autumn, and there can be little doubt but that at least 100 are killed each year on Exmoor. We recall seeing three cross the road at great speed near Wootton Courtenay, when there would have been no chance of avoiding them had we been a little closer. Given satisfactory conditions of food and safety badgers live for about ten years in the wild, and captive ones have lived up to twice this age.

Badgers like to be near a regular source of food, and probably that is why a lot of setts are found not far from houses or farms. Certainly they forage in many gardens and, for the past two years, we have had nightly visits from them. A big boar arrives every evening shortly after dusk, often with a companion, and in the summer months a couple of young ones also come along for the spread of wholemeal bread, peanuts, and scraps of cheese, meat and cake. The big boar always dominates the proceedings and, though all usually feed peacefully, he sometimes swings round suddenly and with a blow from his heavy rump sends an unwelcomed intruder flying. We notice he invariably eats the peanuts first and pokes around among the pile until he finds them.

The badger's routine is to sleep throughout the day and to emerge cautiously at dusk, sniffing the air to ensure there are no strangers around. Often on dry evenings the first task is to collect a supply of fresh bedding of dry grass or bracken. This is carefully gathered with the front feet and tucked well under the chin before shuffling backwards into the sett. Hay and straw may also be collected for bedding if near at hand; and sometimes in the spring green material like leaves of bluebells, wild daffodils, and dog's mercury. When the claws become clogged or blunted by excavation work on the sett, they are cleaned on a nearby tree, often an elder, leaving obvious scratch marks. Badgers have special places for their latrines, which from our observations are at some distance from the sett, for they are remarkably clean animals.

Once their evening chores are over badgers trot off along well-beaten paths to forage for food. They are true omnivores, eating both plant and animal food. Earthworms and insects make up a large part of the average diet, plus the occasional small mammal and young bird. Gleanings of wheat and barley, fallen plums, apples, and acorns are eaten in the autumn. Wasp nests are dug out for the grubs, and wild bees for honey.

Badger cubs are born early in the year, mainly in February, with three as the normal litter. They remain underground in the sett for about three months suckled by their mother. When first emerging they play around the sett for some weeks, but gradually learn to forage and to extend their nightly excursions which, in adults, can be as much as a mile and a half.

Badgers and their setts are fully protected under the Badger Act, 1973, and the Wildlife and Countryside Act, 1981. The maximum penalty is £1,000 for each offence.

Red Fox

The red fox occurs throughout Europe and is widespread on Exmoor from coastal cliffs to high moorland. It is found on the edge of most villages and towns and regularly moves into them at night to forage around the houses. The various Hunts on Exmoor kill at least 500 foxes a year. Others are shot or snared, yet it still remains common, surviving by native cunning, alertness and skill. 'Crafty as a fox' is an ancient proverb. Although mainly nocturnal, it is frequently about in the daytime hunting for food, or when disturbed from slumber in some lonely spot on the moors.

The fox is unmistakeable in its rich russet coat, white throat, narrow muzzle, prominent erect ears, and long bushy tail or brush often tipped white. It feeds mainly on mice, voles and rabbits, supplemented with eggs, beetles, earthworms, and household scraps with fruits and berries in the autumn. Hens and ducks, and weakling lambs may also be taken, and a fox has been known to kill a cat, though this is very rare. Surplus food is often buried, and we have seen a rabbit disposed of in this way.

The fox is not an energetic digger and usually takes over a rabbit burrow which it enlarges; or it may move in for a time with a badger. The bark of a dog fox is much like that of a dog, and the mid-winter mating cry of the vixen is an eerie, piercing scream. Cubs, usually four or five to a litter, are born in the earth or burrow in the spring and remain with the vixen until the autumn. They are very playful, and often come out in the daytime to frisk and gambol around their earth.

Otter

Well adapted for an aquatic life with a water-repellent fur and webbed feet, the otter survives on Exmoor only in small numbers. Thirty years ago it was relatively common, but since then there has been a general decline in numbers all over Britain, due mainly to river pollution and the clearing of bushes and rushes from banks. However, there are stretches of Exmoor waters still travelled by dog otters, and quiet spots where a female makes a

Playful fox cubs by their earth.

David Doble

'holt' and her cubs are born. The few occasions when we have seen them have been red-letter days indeed!

The adult otter is about three feet long, its fur a dark slate-brown except for a white chin patch. The tail is thick and tapering, the ears and eyes small. In the water it swims and dives with great agility. It should not be confused with the alien mink which is widespread along Exmoor streams but only half the size of an otter, usually dark bronze in colour sometimes with cream patches, and a short cat-like tail.

Eels make up a large part of the otter's diet together with a range of other fish from sticklebacks to salmon, and more rarely frogs and young birds. We have discreetly followed an otter for half-a-mile down a moorland water as it searched overhanging banks for likely food. Their presence is best detected by droppings or 'spraints' made up largely of fish scales and bones, and by the seals or footprints in sandy edges of streams with five toes arched around the pad. Otters are now fully protected at all times, and otter hounds that sometimes visit Exmoor now hunt mink.

Weasel and Stoat

These are the two smallest of the British carnivores, and both are fairly common over much of Exmoor. That they are not frequently seen is because they hunt mainly at dusk and dawn, keep closely to hedgerows, and on the high moor to stone and turf walls and rocky outcrops. While sitting in our car late one afternoon near the dovecote at Blackford, a weasel looked out from the hedge, peered around, and then dashed across the road followed by four young and another adult. We have also seen them near Larkbarrow, and running across roads from the outskirts of Minehead to Simonsbath. Judging by the number of road casualties the stoat is more common than the weasel.

An adult weasel is about eight inches long, with a short tail of only two inches. It is a rich reddish-brown above and white below, with a small head and a body so slim it can easily enter mouse holes. Field mice and bank voles form its main food which it finds in hedgerows, but it will kill rats, ground-nesting birds, and more rarely rabbits. It is reckoned that a family of weasels will account for 2,000 rodents a year.

The stoat is the larger, stouter animal, about twelve inches long, with a furry tail of five inches tipped black. Its coat is warm brown above, creamy-white below, and the short legs give it a sleek, muscular appearance. The stoat kills its victims by a bite at the back of the neck, and takes rabbits, mice, voles, and less frequently birds.

Brown Hare and Rabbit

The brown hare is a native of Great Britain, and its name is Saxon, meaning 'the jumper'. It is found in most of Europe and Africa down to the Cape of Good Hope and this is reflected in its scientific name *Lepus capensis*. The rabbit was introduced into England for its meat and fur by the Normans around the year 1200. At first it was confined within mounds or warrens, but it must quickly have become a pest for a charter, granted to the burgesses of Dunster in 1254, stated that 'if any find a rabbit hurtful to them they shall kill it, and bring the skin to the castle'. Conygar Tower on the edge of Dunster and the Warren just east of Minehead are reminders of these early rabbit holdings.

Wild rabbits did not become common in the English countryside until the middle of the 17th century when greatly improved grassland and some newly-introduced winter crops provided it with better feeding. It is reckoned that five rabbits will eat as much as one sheep. The rabbit is smaller than the hare, lives in colonies usually below ground, and the young are born blind and naked. Huge numbers died in the myxomatosis epidemics of 1955 and 1956. The disease is now endemic, it comes and goes, still kills many, but more and more rabbits survive each year so that they are now becoming common again over much of Exmoor.

There are two species of hares in Great Britain, the brown hare and the smaller mountain hare which occurs only in the highlands of Scotland and all of Ireland. Small numbers of brown hares live throughout the National Park, on the Brendons, the coastal marshes, and on the heather moors. Apart from the mating season when the 'Mad March Hare' dashes about at all hours, it is mainly a solitary creature. It lives above ground in a shelter of thick grass, gorse or heather, known as a 'form'. The young, called leverets, are born with a complete coat of fur, open eyes, and active. In five weeks they are quite independent.

The hare plays a large part in local folklore with wise women in moorland villages turning themselves into white hares. There was an occasion when one was shot but escaped. The next day the local wise woman was seen limping—but white hares are very rare nowadays!

Squirrels

Two species of squirrels are resident in Britain, the native red squirrel, and the American-introduced grey squirrel. Their name comes to us through the ancient Greek, meaning 'shady tail'. The red squirrel has alas disappeared from Exmoor, but the grey now lives in almost every wood and park, and frequently visits gardens in search of food. A decline in the red squirrel population was noted even before the First World War, but it remained fairly common until the hard winter of 1947. Thereafter numbers rapidly dwindled until ten years later it had vanished from Exmoor, probably the result of disease combined with a shortage of pine seeds, its staple food. Sometimes we get reports of red squirrels on Exmoor, but these are almost certainly the grey which often has a bronze stripe down each side. Red squirrels can still be seen on the Isle of Wight, the tip of Cornwall, Norfolk, North Wales, northern England and Scotland. In some of these places the two squirrels often overlap and follow a fairly peaceful co-existence.

The grey squirrel arrived on Exmoor in 1950, and is a larger and more aggressive animal than the red. Its main food consists of acorns and hazelnuts which it weighs in a paw, rejecting the lighter ones without a kernel. The shell is nipped by the teeth and then split neatly in half down the cleavage. The diet also includes soft fruit, fungi, and sap from the inner bark of trees, especially the sycamore. They live in oval 'dreys', each the size of a rugby ball placed securely in trees. These have an inner lining of grass, moss, wool and feathers, with leafy twigs on the outside, and are used for sleeping, shelter, and as nurseries with usually five to a litter. They can swim well. Recently we saw one jump into the flooded Horner Water and cross safely to the opposite bank, though it was carried some thirty yards downstream. The tail was stretched out flat on the water, and it emerged apparently quite dry before trotting off into the undergrowth. Squirrels do not hibernate and are active on most days of the year.

Hedgehog

This is the largest of the Insectivores, an Order that includes the mole and the shrews. In common with bats and the dormouse it hibernates in the winter months, though it often wakes up after a week or so and turns over, or in mild spells will spend an hour or two trundling around. In the old days it was called an 'urchin', and in West Somerset dialect a 'fuzz-pig'.

Hedgehogs live mainly in deciduous woodland, thick hedgerows and big gardens where they devour most pests. We know of folk who regard them as free-ranging pets and find they come regularly at dusk for food. They usually live in a dry nest of grass and leaves and range over a territory of about half-a-square mile. An adult hedgehog is twelve inches long, and weighs 1½lbs., but a well fed semi-domesticated one can reach three to four pounds. The four or five young are born in June, and after two weeks have well developed spines and fur. At four weeks they begin to forage

17

around with the mother. With the loss of hedgerows and grass fields turned to arable, the hedgehog has declined over much of England. Even on Exmoor numbers have gone down in recent years, perhaps due to the increase of motor traffic.

Mole

This six-inch mammal clad in a soft velvet fur is both widespread and common over much of Exmoor apart from the high moor. Malmsmead in Doone country was 'Moles-Mead' in 1800. In northern England it is called 'Mouldiwarp', an Old English name meaning 'earth thrower'. Locally it is known as a 'wont'. The mole lives mainly in underground tunnels, and with only small eyes can probably just about tell day from night. It has no visible ears, but the pink snout is remarkably sensitive and is the chief organ for detecting earthworms. 'The mole has no need of a lantern', is an old country saying.

Molehills are formed during tunnel construction with the main system six inches underground, plus others only just below the surface. These are patrolled regularly to pick up the earthworms that drop into them. When the latter become scarce fresh tunnels are added to the system. Apart from the mating season individual moles keep much to themselves. The normal litter is four born in April, the young becoming independent by autumn. The lifespan of a mole is about three years and the British population has been estimated at four per acre. That gives Exmoor a population of around half-a-million.

Dormouse

This plump five-inch-long animal is neither a true mouse nor a miniature squirrel, but has a place midway between the two. It is a most appealing little creature with big dark eyes, a rich tawny fur, long black whiskers, and a furry tail. Unfortunately it is almost entirely nocturnal, feeds in thick bushes and undergrowth, and hibernates for six months of the year. Thus it is rarely seen, and is confined largely to southern England where it is sometimes known as the 'seven-sleeper'.

Various animals feed on hazel nuts; squirrels split them neatly in half; jays and nuthatches make a jagged hole to get at the kernel; field mice and bank voles leave clearly defined teeth marks round the inside edge of the hole; but dormice make a neat circular opening on one side of the nut, leaving a very smooth inside edge. As dormice feed up in the branches the discarded shells are dropped down in a haphazard fashion, and we have found them among dead leaves in many parts of Exmoor. We have also found dormice hibernating in nest boxes. For several years we campaigned for their greater protection under the law, and were delighted when this was granted in 1988. The dormouse has a relatively long lifespan of four years, probably because it spends half of this time asleep.

Shrews, Voles, Mice

Shrews are small creatures with long thin snouts that feed on earthworms, spiders and insects. The smallest member of the family, the pygmy shrew, is quite common on Exmoor, but the common shrew is less abundant. It makes runs in grass and other close-knit vegetation and bustles to and fro both night and day, pausing only for a short spell to sleep. When two meet up they invariably quarrel, so much so that the first definition of 'shrew' in the *Concise Oxford Dictionary* is 'A scolding woman'. The larger, slate-coloured water shrew is quite rare and has only been recorded around Porlock and Minehead.

Voles are distinguished by their blunt, rounded heads and short tails. The water vole (the water rat in Kenneth Grahame's book, *The Wind in the Willows*) is the largest and scarcest of the three voles which occur on Exmoor. The other two are the bank vole and field vole, both of which have many natural predators in the kestrel, owl, weasel, stoat and young foxes. Voles are almost entirely vegetarians.

The wood mouse or long-tailed field mouse and house mouse are both common, and the tiny harvest mouse rather scarce. The wood mouse often moves into barns and houses during autumn and may take up permanent residence. The harvest mouse lives in the bottom of hedges, long grass, cornfields and reed beds. For the summer it builds a globular nest of grass often lined with thistle down, but in the winter it seeks refuge in tussocks and bales of hay and straw. Food is mainly seeds, wild fruits, and a few insects.

Bats

These belong to an Order of furry mammals called *Chiroptera,* meaning 'hand-winged'. In flight it can twist and turn more efficiently than most birds, giving rise to the country name of 'flittermouse'. In West Somerset it was always called the 'leathern bird'. Bats feed chiefly at dusk and dawn on insects which they catch with the aid of their remarkable powers of echolocation, a natural form of radar. On Exmoor the pipistrelle is the most common, also the smallest weighing only ½ oz. We know of colonies in house roofs of up to 200. The long-eared bat is also fairly common, and for some years we have watched over a roost of 30 lesser horseshoe bats together with a few greater horseshoe bats. These latter are among the rarest in Britain. Other bats we have identified include Daubenton's or the water bat, whiskered bat, Natterer's bat, and the noctule bat, the largest of our bats with a wing-span of 15 inches.

Female bats have a single young born in mid-summer and, for the first two weeks, it clings to the mother when she sallies out at dusk. After this she hangs it up in a safe place, and by the autumn it can fly freely. Their life span is about six years, but a few marked bats have been known to live up to 20 years. Bats hibernate in winter when their food supply is almost non-existent. All bats are fully protected, and advice on how to deal with bats in houses should be obtained from the Nature Conservancy Council, whose local address is in the telephone directory.

Amphibians and Reptiles

Amphibians start life in water, first as eggs, then as tadpoles, but in the adult stage spend much of their time on land. Britain has only six native species of amphibians and five of these occur on Exmoor, the frog, toad, crested newt, palmate newt, and smooth newt. Exmoor has a good frog population and from February onwards the spawn can be found in almost every pool and ditch from the coast to the highest parts of the moor. Toads are fairly common but are generally found below 800 feet. They are learned too, for we recently found one in Alcombe Bookshop! The small palmate newt is widespread and we often come across it in moorland pools, but the crested and smooth newts are both quite scarce and confined to the lower parts of Exmoor.

Like the amphibians, six native reptiles also occur in Britain, with four on Exmoor, the adder or viper, grass snake, slow-worm, and common lizard. Adders come out of hibernation near the end of March and are active until the autumn. We have seen them basking on sunny days up to the middle of November. The usual background colour of the male is grey with a distinct black zig-zag pattern along the full length of the back. Females are larger and more variable in colour; often reddish during the first year, becoming browner when mature, but with the same zig-zag stripe. Jet black adders are not unusual on Exmoor, and most conspicuous when sunning themselves amid heather and dead bracken in April. Grass snakes are uncommon in the National Park, and are usually reported from damp areas along the coast and in the lower valleys. Adults are about three feet long, about twice the length of adders, olive-green in colour with a series of black oblong dots along both sides and with two

Slow-worm, NOT a snake but a legless lizard.

Peter Davis

yellow patches behind the head. Grass snakes are quite harmless, but adders have a poisonous bite. It is, however, rare to be bitten as adders normally slip away quickly when approached.

The slow-worm occurs frequently over much of Exmoor, and although it looks like a thin, copper-coloured snake, it is a harmless, legless lizard. The five-inch long common lizard is found most often in dry patches of grass, heather, and in among stone walls.

Freshwater Fish

Exmoor is famous for its trout streams, where the native brown trout provide sport for the fisherman. In the summer months there are runs of sea trout and salmon journeying from the sea to their spawning grounds in the upper river reaches. Elvers, young eels, nearing the conclusion of their three-year journey from the North Atlantic, sometimes occur in thousands. Reservoirs and fish farms are stocked with rainbow trout which occasionally escape. Bullheads lurk beneath stones in the larger rivers. In still waters, tench and stickleback (three-, ten- and fifteen-spined) provide interest for small boys. River lampreys are scarce and stone loach very rare—since Jan Ridd caught them all, according to R. D. Blackmore!

For further information on this subject, on river wildlife, and the sport of fishing, the reader is referred to Noel Allen's Microstudy, *The Waters of Exmoor* (Exmoor Press, £1.50).

21

Male Stonechat on gorse.

G. H. E. Young

3 *Bird Life*

Birds on Exmoor can be divided into five main groups:

Residents that are found throughout the year, e.g. robins, song thrushes, dippers and buzzards.

Summer Residents which come to Exmoor in the spring to nest and rear their young and depart in the autumn. These include the warblers, swallows, and auks.

Winter Visitors arriving in the autumn from colder parts of the British Isles and Continental Europe, fieldfare, brambling, woodcock, and turnstone are regular winter visitors.

Passage Migrants that pass through Exmoor and usually only stop for a few days to rest and feed. Many waders, terns, white and yellow wagtails are annual migrants.

Rare Birds only occur at irregular intervals and comprise a variety of birds from avocet to waxwing. Only those which have been reliably reported on Exmoor over the past ten years are mentioned.

Residents

With 80 different species these make up the largest group of Exmoor's birds and range from the mute swan, the largest British bird, to the goldcrest, the smallest in Europe. Some like the kingfisher, merlin, and redshank are rare with less than five breeding pairs. On the other hand the blue tit, blackbird, and wren are common and widespread from the coast to the high moorland villages of Withypool and Simonsbath. However, many resident birds are relatively limited in their range, and so we have grouped them under five main habitats:

Village and Farmland

Here we find many of our most familiar birds: robins, chaffinches, greenfinches, house sparrows, dunnocks or hedge sparrows, starlings and blackbirds. They are all common enough, and yet each species has an interesting story to tell. The wren, for example, is the smallest of our brown coloured birds, with a loud boisterous song, and a short direct flight on whirling wings. In the springtime the male is a busy bird. He builds three or four domed nests which are inspected in turn by the female, who selects one and then finishes it off with a lining of feathers. During the winter spare nests are often used as community roosts with as many as 20 wrens crowding in for warmth and shelter. Though a regular garden bird the wren rarely feeds off bird tables, for its main diet is insects which it searches out in dense vegetation such as brambles, nettle beds, ivy, and bracken.

Six different tits are resident on Exmoor. The blue and great tits are regular garden birds though they often move away into woods to breed. During the winter many are dependent on nuts and fat which are often put out for them. It is reckoned that 14 million homes in Great Britain feed wild birds, and that the population would be reduced by half without this help when natural food is scarce. The coal tit is the smallest member of the family and is frequently found in conifer plantations, but also in gardens. Marsh and willow tits are less common and not easy to distinguish one from the other. Both are brownish birds with black caps, that of the marsh tit being more glossy, and there is a difference in the call-note. Until 1900 even expert ornithologists had not distinguished between the two. The long-tailed tit is a master builder, and in two weeks constructs a mar-vellous oval nest of moss bound with hair and cobwebs, lined with hun-dreds of feathers and decorated on the outside with lichens. The entrance hole is normally made in the side of the nest but once we saw one with the hole on the top. Apart from the long-tailed tit the rest of the family are hole-nesters, while the blue and great tit readily take to nest boxes. All lay big clutches of 10 to 14 eggs and are single-brooded.

In recent years the crow family have not only moved nearer to villages but often right into them. We have had a crow nesting on our chimney; magpies have built their bulky stick nest two years running in a neighbour's apple tree; and several people who installed central heating and blocked up their fireplaces now have jackdaws as lodgers in their chimneys! Rooks seem to have a preference for human company, and many villages and farms have rookeries. Perhaps the largest with over 100 nests is in Roadwater, and the highest at over 1,000 feet must be at Simonsbath.

Pheasants, grey and red-legged partridges are bred as game birds by shooting syndicates in various parts of Exmoor. Some birds have escaped to live freely on farmland and rough hillsides as at Alcombe Common and on Ley Hill above Porlock. The grey partridge is indigenous and keeps to the lower arable and grass fields but is rather scarce. The red-legged is more abundant and widespread especially in the Brendon Hills. It was introduced from France as long ago as 1790 and is sometimes called the 'French partridge'.

The spread of the collared dove into Britain and Exmoor has been remarkable — probably the bird feat of the century. In 1930 it began moving westwards from the eastern fringe of Europe finding a niche wherever grain was available, on docksides, around mills, and in corn fields. By 1955 it was nesting in England, and reached Exmoor in 1963. Now it is common in all the villages and hamlets, and we have counted a flock of 50 on telephone wires near Dunster. Only two white eggs are laid in a flimsy nest of twigs, but a pair may have three or four broods a year.

The handsome bullfinch is rarely seen apart from his more subdued mate slipping along hedgerows or devouring fruit buds. In the winter small parties often visit the moors to eat heather seed. The yellowhammer is another of Exmoor's more colourful residents with a bright yellow head and underparts. This is also a bird of the hedgerows, especially in the Porlock Vale and the Brendons, and on open hillsides up to 1,000 feet. A related bird is the cirl bunting, told by its black throat and eyestripe and greenish band across the yellow breast. However, it is very scarce, with only a few pairs breeding in sheltered corners between Porlock and Minehead.

Woodland

Many birds that live chiefly in woodland throughout the year often nest in holes also used as regular sleeping quarters. Among them are the three woodpeckers, nuthatch, treecreeper, tawny owl, jackdaw, and stockdove. Other residents of the woods include the buzzard, jay, wood pigeon, and mistle thrush.

The green and yellow green woodpecker is the largest member of its family, and frequently wanders away from woods in search of ants, its favourite food. For this purpose it often turns up on lawns, especially in the early morning. Its loud laughing call is a familiar sound along the edges of woods and overgrown hedges, and even high up on the moor as at Larkbarrow and Tom's Hill. Its country name of 'yaffle' is a supposed imitation of its cry, but this sounds much more like, 'quee-quee-quee-quee-quee'. The two other woodpeckers, the great spotted and lesser spotted, both drum on trees, usually dead branches, to make known their territories in March and April. This drumming consists of a series of short, rapid two-second bursts and can be heard for upwards of a hundred yards. If a house is in a quiet situation, the great spotted woodpecker will come for peanuts and also bring its young along. It is twice the size of the lesser spotted, much more common, but both occur in nearly all our big woods. The three woodpeckers all excavate a fresh nest hole each spring, the old ones usually being taken over by nuthatches, starlings, or the summer-visiting pied flycatchers and redstarts. Like many hole-nesting birds, the four to six eggs are white.

Among woodland birds the nuthatch and treecreeper are the most wed-ded to trees, though the nuthatch will sometimes wander off to feed on nuts at bird tables. Its presence is often revealed by a resounding call of 'pee-pee-pee-pee', and by its habit of wedging hazel nuts into the bark of trees, which it then hacks open to get at the kernel. Hence its old name of 'nut-hack'. A sparse nest is made in holes of trees, and sometimes in wall cavities and nest boxes. The entrance is plastered with mud until a hole of 1½ inches across is achieved. Nuthatches at Treborough have also plas-tered up any cracks in the joints of next boxes they use.

Treecreepers are brownish, mouse-like birds that creep up tree trunks by a series of short jerks in search of insects. When the top is reached they fly down to the bottom of the next tree to start another upward journey. This is unlike the nuthatch which moves freely both up and down. Both are fairly common in most of Exmoor's deciduous woods. Treecreeper nests are built in cracks of branches, behind loose bark, in ivy, and we have found them wedged at the back of notice boards nailed to trees.

A notable resident of our woodlands is the tawny owl, also known as the brown or wood owl. It is largely nocturnal and in the winter often roosts in holly trees from which we have accidentally disturbed it in the daytime. Eggs are usually laid in holes of trees, but we have seen them in an old raven's nest, and grey, young owlets perched in oaks at Cloutsham. It has also nested recently in Blenheim Gardens in the middle of Minehead. The call is the well known 'hoot', usually repeated two or three times, 'hoo-hoo-hoo', from January to June. The little owl is not very common but occurs in the Porlock Vale and elsewhere on the lower parts of Exmoor with old hedgerows and scattered farmsteads.

To watch five or six buzzards circling effortlessly over moor and combe is indeed a grand sight, with their broad wings, 'fingered at the tips' and four feet across, held just above the horizontal. The brown and white under-pattern varies greatly, and some are very pale on the breast. In wooded country the plaintive mewing cry is often the first indication that they are about. Numbers suffered a dramatic fall in 1955 when myx-omatosis in rabbits killed off their main source of food, and they had to turn to mice, voles and birds. As rabbits have slowly increased again so has the buzzard, and the Exmoor population is back to well over a hundred pairs. The sparrow hawk suffered a similar calamity in the mid 1960s due to the build-up of toxic chemicals, but this too has recovered and is common again. It is often an unwelcome visitor to gardens where it takes tits, sparrows and blackbirds, and we have seen it plucking a collared dove, and even known it to carry off a green woodpecker.

Fewer birds live in conifer plantations though the goldcrest, coal tit, and sometimes the great spotted woodpecker and treecreeper may be found there. The siskin, a small olive and yellow finch, bred on Exmoor in 1979 in a conifer plantation near Luccombe. This was the first Somerset breeding record, and it has probably nested annually since. During the winter the siskin is a frequent nut feeder and seems partial to those hung in red nets. The crossbill has almost cetainly bred among conifers over the past few years on Croydon Hill, where adults with young have been seen.

Waterside

The rotund dipper with its white chest, chestnut waistband, and dark brown mantle is a popular resident on almost all of Exmoor's fast flowing streams. A pair seem to occupy about a mile of waterway where they feed on aquatic insects and crustaceans. Numbers have been maintained over the years, and they have not been affected by acid waters, as in Wales where many streams flow through vast conifer plantations. The dipper swims well, and walks and even flies under water in pursuit of its food. An unusual feature is a third white eyelid which it flicks sideways, like a windscreen wiper, to clear water off its eyeball. Any careful observer can see this when a dipper stands on a boulder bobbing up and down. It is an early nester with eggs laid in late March in a domed nest of moss and grass, usually constructed under a plank bridge or overhanging bank.

Another bird that loves the rushing waters of Exmoor is the grey wagtail, and pairs seem to haunt the same place for year after year. It has a very long, blackish tail, yellow on the rump and underparts, and very undulating in flight. The male has a black throat and is generally brighter than its mate. Some folk mistake it for the yellow wagtail, but this is a brown and yellow bird, chiefly a migrant along the coast and rarely stays to breed on Exmoor. Our other resident is the black and white pied wagtail often found near water, but seems just as much at home around farms, gardens, and in our narrow lanes.

The cobalt blue and chestnut kingfisher is the most brilliant of all our birds. Only a few pairs nest on Exmoor mainly at Brushford, on the Exe near Winsford, and sometimes on the Avill above Dunster. It needs quiet

Dipper on mid-stream boulder. A resident.

G. H. E. Young

Male Wheatear—a summer visitor.

pools where it can safely dive for small fish. In the autumn kingfishers wander as far as Simonsbath, Porlock and Minehead, where we have seen them fishing in rock pools. The heron is another skilful fisher and whose diet also includes frogs, mice, and sometimes small birds. Its large size makes it conspicuous, but it is, in fact, quite scarce with not above 25 pairs breeding on Exmoor in four small heronries. Moorhen and coot are two rather secretive water birds, and may easily be overlooked. A few pairs nest around Wimbleball Lake, along some coastal dykes, and on ponds in hill country. The mallard also breeds widely on Exmoor, even quite high up by moorland streams and bogs. Since 1982 a pair or two of great crested grebes have nested at Wimbleball.

Moorland

Much of the moorland lies between 1200 and 1600 feet above sea level, and in the winter months it can be bleak, wet, and altogether an inhospitable place for birds. The black grouse was a resident for generations, but started to decline near the end of the 19th century, and finally died out in 1975. Red grouse were introduced to Exmoor soon after 1900, and for some years flourished on heather moorland. However, numbers fell away rapidly after 1980 and now only a few pairs remain on Robin How and Dunkery.

The merlin is the smallest and one of the rarest of British falcons with a few breeding pairs on Exmoor. Though fully protected by law, clutches of eggs are still taken by egg collectors, so we can give no habitat locations, but we do know that broods are raised successfully in most years. Other birds of prey which sometimes nest in trees quite high on the moor include sparrowhawk, buzzard, and kestrel. All of these regularly overfly the moor in search of food.

Snipe and curlew both nest in small numbers on the high ground; the snipe in boggy parts among rushes and grass tufts, the curlew in grass or heather. Its haunting call can be heard in the spring over Dunkery, Codsend Moor, Wilmersham, Hoar Moor and Molland Common. We have also found the lapwing nesting on East Anstey Common and at the top of Colly Water.

Two of the confusing 'little brown birds' of the moor and quite common are the skylark and meadow pipit. Fortunately the skylark is unmistakable for six months of the year with its joyous song poured out as it climbs into the sky. The meadow pipit is a frequent prey of the merlin, and a common foster-parent to the young cuckoo. The stonechat is a delightful bird of sheltered combes, the male smartly dressed with black head, white collar and reddish underparts, the female in sombre brown and white.

Coast

Exmoor's coastline stretches for 30 miles from Minehead to Combe Martin. Here the herring gull is the main resident gull, but its numbers have declined by 50% over the past ten years. They nest on suitable cliffs and rock outcrops in small colonies of up to 20 pairs with total numbers of around 300 pairs. Two old raven nests are regularly used by herring gulls on Culver Cliffs, Minehead. Young birds are dusky brown and it is three years before they obtain adult plumage. Before summer is over the cliffs are deserted in the daytime, when the birds flock to the harbours and beaches of Combe Martin, Lynmouth, and Minehead to feed. Some old birds 'in the know' take up posts in parking areas on Porlock Hill, Dunkery, Brendon Common, and Winsford Hill, to beg a living from motorists.

Other residents restricted to the coast during breeding include a few pairs each of great black-backed gull, cormorant, shag, shelduck, and rather more pairs of the little rock pipit. The shelduck is a patchwork of black, white, and chestnut and nests on Porlock Marsh, and in a few other places where scrub or ivy overhang the cliff face to screen the nesting site. With a wing span of six feet the mute swan is Britain's largest bird, but it is not common on Exmoor with only two or three pairs nesting between Dunster Hawn and Minehead. It is rarely seen elsewhere in the National Park, and it is not common in Britain with only about 5,000 breeding pairs. This is quite small compared with four million house sparrows, five million chaffinches, and seven million blackbirds.

The redshank is well described as the 'Warden of the Marshes', with a noisy alarm call that tells all other birds that humans are about. In south-west England it is a scarce breeder but five pairs usually breed each year on Porlock Marsh together with small numbers of lapwing. All the adult birds vigorously defend their young, mobbing all intruders and calling loudly. Oystercatchers and ringed plover have also nested along the shore, but there have been no recent records.

Two of Exmoor's most spectacular birds, the peregrine falcon and raven nest at five to ten-mile intervals along the coast. All the sites are on vertical cliff faces, and so escape the attention of egg collectors. This bodes well for the birds, for a peregrine's egg can fetch up to £5,000 among some falconers. The deep croak of the raven, and the high pitched repeated 'kek-kek-kek' of the peregrine often draws attention to them as they fly overhead. Ravens also nest at ancestral sites inland, mainly in big beeches, and the four to six eggs are laid by the middle of March. So the young hatch when there is plenty of carrion on the moor, for the end of winter is often the hardest time for both moorland sheep and wildlife. Peregrines feed entirely on other birds, and we have seen them take both domestic and wild pigeons, seabirds, and even a ringed plover. Above Heddon's Mouth one day we watched a peregrine swooping down on every passing crow, and then turning away at the last moment. Fun, no doubt, for the peregrine, but alarming for the crows!

Summer Residents

Twenty-four species of birds return to Exmoor each year to nest after wintering in various parts of Africa. Another four winter out on the ocean, and a further four are rather rare, breeding only occasionally with us. We call them 'summer visitors' or 'summer residents', but the wheatear and ring ouzel are invariably back on the moor before March is out, and the arboreal chiffchaff and willow warbler are never far behind.

The ring ouzel is a true bird of the uplands, and rarely nests below 1,000 feet. Its local name is 'mountain colly', and there are place names like Colly Water and Colly Hill. In appearance it is much like a blackbird but with a white crescent blazoned on its breast, and a greyish tinge to its dark plumage. It is not common, only about 30 pairs breed on the high moor from the upper reaches of Hoar Oak Water below the Chains, to Hannycombe on Robin How. The wheatear is more abundant, also more obvious for it delights to perch on rocks, ruined buildings, and stone walls, from lonely places along the coast to the old boundary wall running from Saddle Gate to Black Barrow. The cuckoo and the whinchat are two other regular summer visitors to the lower slopes and sheltered combes of the moor. The cuckoo returns about 17 April, the female laying eggs mainly in meadow and tree pipits' nests.

Exmoor's woodlands and copses attract nine different summer birds. Three of them, chiffchaff, willow warbler, and wood warbler are small olive green birds, but fortunately their song is quite different and this makes identification easy. The wood warbler is the last to arrive towards the end of April, and its two-part song, a series of clear single notes that accelerate into a trill, are heard in almost every deciduous wood throughout May and June. Blackcap and garden warbler are fine songsters, their song much alike, but the blackcap's is rather fuller and the bursts shorter. Neither are easy to see for they love to perform from the middle of thick hedgerows or dense bushes.

Two handsome summer visitors are the male pied flycatcher and the redstart. The pied flycatcher first nested in Somerset in the Horner Woods and the population in 1968 was about 30 pairs, but today nearer 200 pairs. It breeds in most broad-leaved woods and takes readily to nest boxes. Honeysuckle bark is always included in the nesting material. The redstart is more widespread and usually nests in holes in trees, stone walls, and banks. Whitethroats are fairly common along the older hedgerows, and on open heaths with gorse and hawthorn, but the lesser whitethroat is a very scarce visitor. Sometimes the grasshopper warbler occurs in a similar habitat.

The turtle dove is another scarce visitor, but a few pairs arrive most years to spend the summer in the Brendon Hills. We have seen it on telegraph wires near Treborough, and heard its lovely soft purring call 'turr-turr-turr' on the outskirts of Dunster and Timberscombe. A rather unusual visitor is the night-flying nightjar which has vanished from many parts of Britain but still returns annually to Exmoor. Croydon Hill, Grabbist, Hawkcombe, and around Webber's Post are some of its favourite places, and where its long churring call and liquid whistle can be heard at dusk in June and July.

Early swallows and house martins return to our villages and farms during the first week of April. Swifts rarely appear before the end of the month, and are the first to leave for Africa in the last week of August. Swallows and house martins are great travellers and winter 6,000 miles away in South Africa. Pairs usually return to the same nesting site year after year. Spotted flycatchers are indeed great catchers of flies, but only the young birds are spotted. They arrive from Central Africa in late April or early May to take up temporary residence around farms and isolated houses. Most have a favourite perch from which they sally forth after insects and then return to the same spot.

Reed beds are not common on Exmoor, but there is a fairly large one on Porlock Marsh, and several smaller ones near Minehead. These attract a few pairs of reed warblers and sedge warblers and they are best told apart by the clear, white eye stripe of the latter. There has been a general decline in sand martin numbers over the whole of Britain in recent years, and the small Exmoor colonies are no longer occupied apart from one below Dulverton. Apparently they have suffered badly in their winter quarters in drought-stricken parts of Africa.

One of the best seabird colonies in south-west England is located on the high cliffs between Lynmouth and Heddon's Mouth. After spending the winter out at sea razorbills, guillemots, fulmars, and kittiwakes gather here to breed. Altogether there are about 350 pairs each of razorbills and guillemots, which have completed nesting by the end of July and soon

Badgers foraging in a
Minehead garden *Noel Allen*

Fox—mealtime at
Alcombe *F. A. Jones*

Red Deer Hind *Graham Floyd*

Black and Grey Adders *Noel Allen*

Young Ring Ouzel

Male Grey Wagtail

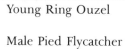

P. G. Deane

Female Redstart among
Maidenhair Spleenwort

Male Pied Flycatcher

Southern-marsh Orchid

Caroline Giddens

Bog Asphodel   *Olive Russell*

White Mullein— Yellow variety

Moonwort Fern   *Noel Allen*

Green Hairstreak Butterfly

Heath Fritillary Butterfly

Noel Allen

Broad-bodied Libellula Dragonfly

Emperor Moth Caterpillar

leave for the sea again. Fulmars arrived here in 1958 and now there are some 250 pairs with smaller colonies near Combe Martin and at Glenthorne. The last to come were kittiwakes with five pairs in 1973, which have built up to over 200 pairs along this four-mile stretch of coast.

Three other summer birds are somewhat sporadic visitors to Exmoor. The nightingale nests on the border between Old Cleeve and Washford and sometimes wanders a mile or two to sing around Carhampton and Dunster. In the Porlock Vale the 'wet-my-lips' call of the quail is heard at intervals, and almost certainly nests some years in the barley fields. The hobby, a dashing falcon that winters in Central Africa, is seen from time to time, but so far there has been no evidence that it nests on Exmoor. It is rare over the whole of Britain with no more than a hundred breeding pairs.

So our summer birds spread out into every part of Exmoor, from the coast to the high moors where they add so much colour, life, and interest to the wildlife scene.

Winter Visitors

Birds that move down to over-winter on Exmoor arrive from many European countries as well as from northern Britain. Among the waders turnstones travel from Iceland (they do turn stones over on the beaches for marine creatures), sanderling from the Arctic, ringed plover, dunlin, curlew and oystercatchers from northern Britain. The earliest of these are back on the beaches by mid-August, together with black headed gulls and common gulls.

It is usually October before the majority of the wild duck appear when there are mallard, widgeon, shelduck, shoveler and teal off Minehead and Dunster, and in Porlock Bay and on the marshes. Occasional duck include pintail, gadwall, common scoter, and goosander. Wimbleball Lake is the only reservoir on Exmoor to attract large numbers of winter visitors. The late autumn attracts widgeon up to 600, teal to 200, pochard and tufted duck to 50, and small numbers of goldeneye, goosander, gadwall, and shoveler. There are also several hundred coot and a dozen little grebes. Geese are irregular winter visitors depending much on the severity of the weather in north and east England. Brent geese, barnacle, and white-fronted, turn up in most years. Apart from the resident mute swan, other wild swans are rare and only the Bewick has been recorded in recent years.

By early October Scandinavian fieldfare and redwing reach the moorland combes to finish off the rowan and hawthorn berries left by our home-based mistle thrushes. When these are finished they move down to lower ground, and feed in the fields with flocks of wintering starlings and lapwings. After the autumn, chaffinches, and often yellowhammers, gather around farm buildings and are sometimes joined by a few brambling. Golden plover visit both the moor and the beaches in small flocks of 20 to 30, while snipe also winter on both high and low ground. Woodcock are solitary visitors, but can be flushed not only from woods but among bushes on the hillsides.

The water rail is always a regular winter visitor, but it is a secretive and lonely bird haunting ditches and damp places with lots of undergrowth. During a severe frosty spell one visited our garden and fed on wholemeal bread. It was amazingly pugnacious, and fiercely chased off all competitors running at them with its long bill thrust forward. Great grey shrike from Russia, hen harrier, short-eared owl, and the red kite from Wales are other occasional visitors to Exmoor in the autumn and winter months.

Passage Migrants

Exmoor is a highway for large numbers of migrant birds; the majority travel northwards in the spring to breed, and return with their young in the late summer and autumn. Some swallows, house martins, warblers, wheatears, common redstarts, and pied flycatchers, drop out of the main stream to nest with us, but the majority pass on to other parts of Britain. In the spring these migrants are generally in a hurry, and only stop for a few hours to feed and rest, but the autumn migration is more leisurely and birds may hang around for weeks or even months.

A lot of migration takes place along the coast where the chief birds are dunlin, sanderling, curlew, sandpipers, whimbrel, ruff, bar-tailed and black-tailed godwits. Stopping-off places are few along Exmoor's rugged coast and birds tend to concentrate on the beach between Minehead and Dunster and on Porlock Marsh. Smaller numbers may be found at Lynmouth, Heddon's Mouth, and Combe Martin. Offshore, Manx shearwater, gannets, and various gulls and skuas move along the Bristol Channel. Common, Arctic, and little tern dive for fish in the sea, and frequently come on to the beaches to rest especially in August and September.

Other birds using the coastal route include white and yellow wagtails, common sandpipers, snow buntings, and black redstarts. Green and wood sandpipers keep mainly to rivers and streams and also visit Wimbleball Lake. The rare osprey has been recorded on passage both along the coast and at inland reservoirs. Another rare, but probably regular migrant

A pair of Ring Ouzels nesting on the high moor.

G. H. E. Young

is the dotterel, a visitor to the high moor around Dunkery, on its way to and from the mountains of Scotland.

Rare Birds

These are more likely to appear during the spring or autumn migrations when birds either wander or are blown off-course. Over the past ten years an average of three species turn up annually which are normally strangers to Exmoor. Golden oriole, hoopoe, corncrake, and red-backed shrike are occasionally reported in April and May; and wryneck, shore lark, waxwing, and Lapland bunting in the autumn.

Unusual gulls recently identified by experienced birdwatchers include Mediterranean gull, Sabine's gull, laughing gull, and the little gull. Wimbleball lake has attracted black-throated diver, American widgeon, and ruddy duck, and may well attract more rarities in the future. Porlock Marsh is the most regular place for sightings of rare birds with records of little egret, avocet, bittern, grey phalarope, water pipit, Terek sandpiper, blue-winged teal, black-necked grebe, and a pair of eider duck which stayed for much of 1987. Other vagrants seen on Exmoor include marsh and Montagu's harriers, goshawk, rough-legged buzzard, long-eared owl, Dartford warbler, Alpine swift, and hawfinch and wood lark both of which nested on Exmoor 20 years ago.

To see and identify a rare bird is always a bonus, but our resident birds, summer and winter visitors make up the bread and butter of birdwatching. There is always something new and exciting to discover about all of them, whether it is a song thrush nesting in heather near the top of Dunkery Beacon, or a redstart, nuthatch, and pied flycatcher taking up residence in adjacent trees in the Horner Woods.

4 Some Insects and Other Creepy-Crawlies

Insects are so numerous that most are beyond the scope of this book. On Exmoor there have been recorded 16 species of dragonflies, 15 grasshoppers, 1 earwig, 15 plant lice, 254 bugs, 12 lacewings, 42 butterflies (including 5 casuals), 851 moths, 203 flies etc., 80 ants, bees, wasps and 262 beetles; a total of 1751 species and there are hundreds more yet to be identified.

Dragonflies

Although among the fiercest of our insects, Dragonflies are quite harmless to man and country names such as 'Horse-stinger' are quite unwarranted. They have no stings and only other insects on which they prey need fear their snapping jaws. There are two Sub-Orders, the Damselflies which (mostly) close their wings vertically and the true Dragonflies which rest with wings open horizontally and can fly at very high speeds. These are divided again into hawkers which hunt to-and-fro and devour their prey on the wing, and darters which watch from a perch and dash out on their victims. We have often watched a female egg-laying — bobbing up and down over a marsh, dipping her tail-end under when each egg is laid. The brownish nymphs live submerged for one to two years. At this stage Damselflies can be separated by their three 'tails" which are actually breathing gills. Then comes the miraculous change when one day the nymph will climb the stem of a water plant. The back splits and gradually the *imago* emerges. The crumpled wings lengthen and harden, the colours develop slowly and away it flies. One morning we found a common darter by a garden pond, newly emerged, but its fore and hind wings on one side were stuck together. After gentle separation and another hour drying out, it flew off.

The larger Dragonflies on Exmoor are the Broad-bodied *Libellula* greenish Southern hawker, common hawkers, blue emperor and golden ringed. Medium-sized darters include reddish common sympetrum and more rarely black darters. The jewel-like colours of the smaller Damselflies glitter between reeds in summer. Metallic blue-black Agrions are fairly common and others are azure, blue, red and emerald.

Butterflies and Moths

Butterflies and moths belong to the Order of insects known as *Lepidoptera*, from the Greek 'scale wings'. Butterflies fly by day, moths mainly by night. Some 65 species of butterflies have been recorded in Britain, and 37 (excluding the 5 casuals) of these on Exmoor. They have four life stages: egg, caterpillar, chrysalis and the adult. Their main problem is getting through our English winters, and only four survive as adults: small tortoiseshell, peacock, comma, and brimstone; all are common on Exmoor apart from the rather scarce brimstone. Most of the rest live out the winter months as caterpillars, but the red admiral, painted lady and clouded yellow rarely survive in any stage. Exmoor numbers of these three are dependent each year on migrants from the Mediterranean area.

Together with Roger Butcher, the writers discovered the heath fritillary butterfly on Exmoor in 1982 and have now located over 20 colonies. This is regarded as one of Britain's rarest butterflies. Others that occur occasionally on Exmoor are the white-letter hairstreak, silver studded blue, high brown fritillary and the marsh fritillary.

The full list of Exmoor butterflies is:—

The Browns: Speckled Wood, Wall brown, Marbled White, Grayling, Hedge Brown, Meadow Brown, Small Heath, Ringlet.

The Fritillaries: Small Pearl-bordered Fritillary, Pearl-bordered Fritillary, Dark Green Fritillary, High Brown Fritillary, Silver-washed Fritillary, Marsh Fritillary, Heath Fritillary.

The Vanessids: Red Admiral, Painted lady, Small Tortoiseshell, Peacock, Comma.

The Blues: Silver-studded Blue, Common Blue, Holly Blue.

The Coppers: Small Copper.

The Hairstreaks: Green Hairstreak, Purple Hairstreak, White-letter Hairstreak.

The Whites: Large White, Small White, Green-veined White, Orange Tip.

The Yellows: Pale Clouded Yellow, Clouded Yellow, Brimstone.

The Skippers: Dingy Skipper, Small Skipper, Large Skipper.

As most moths are night-flying, they are less often seen unless by some accident as when they blunder into a lighted room. The largest European moth, the Deaths-head hawk, with a wingspan of six inches, is a rare immigrant to Exmoor. It can produce an audible squeak if handled. More common are the slightly smaller privet and poplar hawk-moths. On the moors the furry caterpillars of oak eggars, fox and drinker moths are more often seen than the adults, and the green bodied larvae of the emperor moth feeds on heather. Buff tip moths are hard to spot. When at rest with wings rolled, the cream coloured head exactly resembles a broken twig. Speckled yellow is a common small yellow day-flying moth often mistaken for a butterfly. The red and black cinnabars and six-spot burnets also fly by day. The hundreds of small micro-moths need expert identification

41

and even the larger ones are not always easy. Recently we approached a brown speckled specimen at rest on the house wall and, book in hand, began to scan the illustrations when whoosh! — it was snatched and devoured by a blue-tit! There are probably over a thousand types of moths to be found on Exmoor.

Crickets and Grasshoppers

The most abundant grasshopper in heathland is the mottled grasshopper. The 'song' produced by the male resembles the winding of a clock and lasts approx. twelve seconds. Grasshoppers can be identified by their songs in the same manner as can birds. Other familiar grasshoppers are the common green, the lesser marsh, the field and the meadow. The great green bush-cricket's 'song' is likened to a sewing machine with short breaks every few seconds. This three-inch long species can nip quite hard. The oak bush-cricket is common in deciduous woods. Groundhoppers are like small grasshoppers but silent.

Flies

In most people's opinion one fly is one too many, but next time one falls into your picnic, reflect that here is one of Nature's unexplained miracles. The common blue-bottle begins life as a maggot which pupates after a week's feeding. Within the pupal case it breaks down to a creamy substance which changes and emerges as a fly in about ten days. In less than three weeks the whole process can repeat itself. It is only the thousands that are consumed every day by bats and birds that prevent us from being over-run with flies and other insects. Within the Order of *Diptera* (two-winged flies) come gnats, craneflies, midges, soldier-flies, robber flies, hover-flies and leaf-miners. They are a much understudied group. Caddis flies, mayflies and stoneflies, common near fresh water, are all separate Orders.

Bugs and Beetles

Q. When is a beetle not a beetle? A. When it's a bug! The main difference between bugs and beetles is their feeding habits. Beetles are equipped with biting mouths while bugs have piercing tubes enabling them to suck juices from plants and animals. English names are misleading — the large brown cockchafers locally known as May bugs are beetles, as are ladybirds and glow-worms. Water boatmen and pond skaters are aquatic bugs; cuckoo-spit is produced as a protective covering by the nymphs of froghoppers which are leaping bugs. Shield bugs are attractive little creatures of various colours. Different species are associated with hawthorn, blackthorn, gorse, grasses, birch and other trees. There are many other plant bugs, groundbugs, leafhoppers, etc.

Beetles are the biggest group of insects, and ground beetles, soldier beetles, rove beetles, flower beetles, longhorn beetles and weevils are all well represented on Exmoor. Aquatic species such as diving and whirligig beetles are found in pools. It is impossible to do justice in a few words to this vast group ranging from Tiger beetles — the running champions of the insect world — to the Devil's Coach-horse which raises its tail menacingly when approached. Shiny black dung beetles are frequently encountered and more rarely the red and black sexton beetles will be seen burying carrion. We were amazed at the speed at which they dealt with a dead shrew — shovelling out earth from beneath the body so that it dropped into the hole while we watched. There are black and yellow species of ladybird beetles besides the familiar red ones and the number of spots varies: 2, 4, 7, 11, 14 and 22-spot all occur. Generally popular little insects but not always so. A few years ago we were invaded by swarms from the Continent, and we recall the distress of one hairy chested sunbather who discovered that these invaders were hostile and able to give quite a hard nip!

Ants

About a dozen species of ants have been identified on Exmoor. There are red, yellow and black species — the latter being those that may invade your larder. We recall the horrifying sight of an endless stream: down the garden path, under the back door, across the kitchen, under the larder door, up and into a cupboard wherein stood a bowl of stewed pears! On a sultry, summer day the excited cries of hundreds of seagulls will fill the air — their annual treat is when the flying ants hatch and swarm. These are breeding swarms, workers are all wingless and queens, which start out with wings, break them off as soon as they have laid the foundations of their colony.

Our largest ants are wood ants, often observed struggling across woodland paths with debris several times larger than themselves to build their enormous nests, sometimes three feet high. The small anthills found in grassland are made by yellow meadow ants. *Lasius alienus* is an ant which inhabits *Calluna* moorland.

Bees and Wasps

Buff-tailed bumble bees are a familiar sight labouring among flowers with their burden of pollen to feed the young in their colony. They are essential for the pollination of certain plants e.g. clovers. The nest is in a hole in the ground, often an old mouse-hole. Red-tailed bumble bees are also common and semi-circular pieces missing from leaves, especially roses, denote the presence of leaf-cutter bees, the pieces being used to wrap around their eggs. Small piles of earth mark the entrance to the underground nests of mining bees. Wild honey-bees usually nest in hollow trees, enlarged each year. We remember a fallen ash near Brendon which contained pounds of honeycomb — a treat for badgers which are impervious to stings. Badgers also love the grubs in wasps' nests as we know to our disadvantage. Crossing a scree slope in Horner Valley one day, we spotted the remains of a wasp nest pulled out by a badger. A friend bent down to inspect the papery pieces when suddenly, out of the nest hole issued hundreds of wasps, bent on revenge. Our friend was stung around the head and one of us around the ankles. To make matters worse, the friend had recovered next day but to the less fortunate, socks were unbearable for several weeks. The nests of common wasps are constructed from chewed wood pulp, usually football-sized, but one which was displayed at Malmsmead Field Centre for several years was six times as big. Hornets are large, communal wasps but there are many solitary wasps which build small individual nests from mud.

Sawflies and Ichneumon flies are classified with wasps and there are several which parasitise other insects. There are also many small species which are the 'causers' of plant galls such as Robin's pin-cushion on wild roses, oak-apples, marble galls and spangles on oak. Knopper galls which distort acorns can mean the failure of whole acorn crops, causing a serious food deficiency for birds such as jays. They have increased on Exmoor and elsewhere in recent years.

Other Creepy-Crawlies

There remain a few classes of invertebrate creatures to be described.

Spiders:

Often mistakenly called insects but, as they have eight not six legs, they belong to the Class *Arachnida*. There are well over 200 types on Exmoor. They are a much maligned group which, in Britain, is more beneficial to mankind than otherwise. Their web designs range from the familiar cartwheel shape to the single strand of gossamer, which carries the young spider away from the nest to begin its life. One species makes a web in the form of a tunnel wherein it lies in wait for its prey. The rare water spider spins a bell-shaped web which it fills with air bubbles from the surface for, although it lives entirely underwater, it needs oxygen to breathe. The wolf spider and the striped zebra spider are both hunting spiders which stalk their prey and then pounce. Their silk is used to make protective coverings for their eggs. The thin legged but tiny bodied harvestmen, the *Pseudoscorpiones* and Mites are also classed with spiders.

Worms, Centipedes, Woodlice

There are a dozen or more species of earthworm and, in fresh water, many more flat-, thread- and pot-worms occur. Dozens more are found on beaches. There are about twenty species of *Myriapoda,* the Class which includes centipedes (one pair of legs to each body segment) and millipedes (two pairs). This makes for a lot of legs but nowhere near as many as their names suggest.

To date nine woodlice, which are crustaceans, have been identified on Exmoor. These little creatures have many local names e.g. lucky-pig, cheese-bug and pill-bug. A small white specimen which dwells in red ants' nests was found near Porlock in 1988. They belong to the group known as *Isopoda,* and there are additionally about twelve maritime species, the sea slater being common on the shore.

Molluscs

Exmoor, lacking calcareous soils, is not the best hunting ground for slugs and snails which need a calcium intake for their shells. 'Slugs don't have shells' we hear you say. True for most, and the great black slug *is* abundant on moorland where, after a shower of rain, hundreds emerge to the apparent dismay of many people who seem to have an abhorrence of them. But there is a scarce smaller slug which carries a shell, no larger than a child's finger-nail, on its nether regions. It can be found in well manured gardens.

Snails are hermaphrodite, one being both male and female. After mating, each lays a batch of eggs from which the young snails hatch, complete with shells. Large species take several years to reach maturity. The flattened shell of the discus snails or the tiny spires of door snails enable them to creep into rock crevices. Colours vary from pale yellow, pink, brown and grey with various striped combinations. Albinos can also occur. In fresh water, Jenkins' and wandering snails are common and river limpets are found beneath stones in most Exmoor waters.

Some Coastal Creatures

On the sea shore molluscs of many kinds abound: limpets, cockles, winkles and whelks of various species, and mussel beds at estuaries. Occasionally oyster shells, remains of old oyster beds, are picked up as at Porlock Weir. Chitons are small molluscs with plated shells resembling woodlice dwelling beneath coastal rocks. Barnacles are Crustaceans which encrust rocks and sometimes other shellfish. The stalked goose barnacle occurs in the deeper sea and is very occasionally washed up on driftwood, etc. Its shape, which resembles the head and neck of a barnacle goose, gave rise to the old belief that the migratory birds hatched from these barnacles.

There are many maritime worms, the best known being lug and rag, regularly dug up for bait by fishermen who have to move quickly for they can burrow at an incredible speed. Off Minehead Warren there is a half-mile long reef of the honeycomb-like homes of *Sabellaria* worm which can be seen at very low tide.

Your large bath sponges are Mediterranean species, but several small encrusting sponges grow in the Bristol Channel. These, such as breadcrumb sponge are locally common and grow on stones or sometimes seaweeds or shells. Jellyfish numbers fluctuate from year to year, occasionally large numbers are stranded on a receding tide. In 1987 we watched numerous octopus jellyfish swimming up Channel from High Veer Point. Portuguese Man O'War are very rare, but one was stranded on Minehead Beach in 1976. Beadlet, snakelock and dahlia anemones occupy rock pools, their waving tentacles forming undersea 'flowers', as they reach for small prey to sweep into their central mouths.

Marker buoys, particularly off Lynmouth, indicate where fishermens' lobster pots (usually constructed from old milk crates) have been dropped. Lobsters, crawfish and edible crabs are caught. Prawns are fished from boats and harbour walls, but can also be seen at the edge of the tide. Shrimps and crabs of many varieties abound in rock pools, and sandhoppers where there is rotting sea-weed. By flicking their tails these can hop ten times their own length. Common crabs are protected from many predators by their carapace, a shell-like covering (shed and renewed as the animal grows), but this does not deter crows and gulls generally to be seen poking about for them on the shore. The soft backed hermit crab has no such protection so it inhabits an old shell, usually a whelk's. When it grows it will move house into a larger discarded shell. Starfish, sea urchins, sea gherkins and sea squirts are not often seen but all are present on the less accessible beaches.

5 Plant Life

Plant life on Exmoor ranges from microscopic algae to 100-foot conifers: from annuals which spring up, flower, seed and die in a matter of days to 1000-year-old oaks. It is as diverse in its ways as the animal life. Soil and situation govern what plants grow where, and these in turn determine which animals will be found. Many insects and some birds and beasts are largely dependent on a single species of plant. Some botanical knowledge is essential to any serious naturalist. When we admire the beauty of Exmoor it is plants we are seeing. The changing colours of the seasons are the changing colours of plants. The need for plant conservation is therefore plain. The only natural time that plants are obscured is in snow, but even as the snows melt, the first flowers of the year begin to appear. We have seen primroses in December, lesser celandines on 1st January and snowdrops on the 14th.

For ease of reading, this section is presented under two headings— Flowering and Non-Flowering Plants.

FLOWERING PLANTS

The Woodlands

Within Exmoor National Park there are 6,500 ha (16,500 acres) of woodlands — roughly one tenth of the total area. Of these, around 50% are conifer plantations, 40% ancient or secondary broad-leaved, and 10% mixed and coastal woodlands, some of which are very old. During the last 150 years 1000 ha (2,500 acres) of *ancient* woodland have been lost within the National Park, mainly through felling and conversion to conifer.

Ancient and Secondary Woods

'Ancient woodland' is a term applied to woods which, as far as we know, have been continuously in existence since medieval times, or earlier; possibly survivals of primaeval forest. Woodlands which have grown or been planted since about 1600 are known as 'secondary woodlands'. Apart from reference to historical records or maps which may be available, it is usually possible to determine ancient woodland by the presence of certain indicator plants such as wood anemone or lungwort lichen, but their absence or presence does not alone show the wood's

Horner Woods from Webbers Post. These ancient sessile oak woods are an important site for lichens and bird-life. Scots Pine in foreground.

Mike Barbee

age. The actual number of plants present is also a guide — the longer a wood has been standing, the more species are likely to have come in.

The composition of ancient woodlands varies but the commonest type on Exmoor consists of dominant sessile oak *(Quercus petraea)*, with hazel. Downy birch, ash, rowan and holly are frequent in mixed woodlands and alders grow beside waters in the valley bottoms. English Oak *(Q. robur)* is less common on Exmoor although fine examples can be seen planted in Nettlecombe and Dunster Deer Parks, and in some hedgerows where they provide welcome shade to grazing animals. The English oak can be differentiated from the sessile by its long-stalked acorn cups and leaves with a lobe each side of the stem. Sessile oaks have stemless (sessile) acorn cups and the base of the leaf is V-shaped — but there are many confusing hybrids.

Wych elm, maple, sweet chestnut, wild cherry, whitebeam and spindle occur and, rarely, crab apple. *Pure* stands of ash, birch or holly are rare but are present. Two small English elm stands formerly near Minehead have succumbed to disease, although suckers are still sprouting. As elms regenerate from suckers, not seeds, (producing lots of regional types), future generations may once again see this lovely tree. Beech, although a common hedgerow material, is less common, but it occurs in many mixed woodlands and there are beech plantations, as at Birch Cleave, Simonsbath. The original, natural, birches had been replaced by beech by the Knights by 1840. The National Park Authority purchased the wood in 1973 and are planting and encouraging the regeneration of beeches here where, at 1200 feet, it is one of the highest beech stands in the country.

Coppicing of oak and hazel has taken place in most of the woods. This was the traditional method of management for timber, whereby the tree was cut off near the base from which several new shoots then grew. Much of Horner Wood was last coppiced 70 or 80 years ago, so most trees are of that age, but the stools may be hundreds of years old. The tanning of leather was a local industry which relied on supplies of oak bark. Minehead tanyards, sited where the Regal Cinema is now, closed in the 1930s. Another forestry method was pollarding, which involved cutting off the trunk higher up, so the new growth was out of reach of grazing animals. There are some old pollarded oaks in Hawkcombe and Cloutsham (both areas still frequented by deer), and the National Trust have recently pollarded a few trees to keep up the tradition. Hazel spars had various uses including thatching and hurdle making.

The largest area of ancient woodland remaining on Exmoor is the

Horner Valley complex. Here, the wooded sides of the combes are clothed with sessile oaks over about 300 ha, of which 250 ha are considered ancient. There is surprisingly little ground flora but the woods are of national importance for their lichen flora and bird life.

The Lyn Valley woods come next in size. These cover 570 ha but only 135 ha are classed as ancient. However, Myrtleberry Cleave is perhaps our most interesting region for its variety of flowering plants; also there are some rare species of whitebeam.

Barle Valley Woods (508 ha, 201 ancient) are likewise important and include the Somerset Trust Reserve at Mounsey. This is a most valuable site both for ground flora and lichens, also butterflies. Other woods with 100 ha or more of ancient standing are in the valleys of the Haddeo, Exe/Quarme, Heddon and Hawkcombe Water, and the coastal areas.

Woodland Flowers

Some of these are among the earliest to bloom as light is needed to produce flowers and fruits, and they must 'get on with it' before the leaf canopy comes to cast its shade. The fame of Snowdrop Valley near Timberscombe has already generated a traffic problem, thanks to hundreds of vehicles carrying visitors from nearby towns eager to be convinced in February that spring is on the way. The trampling of so many feet is beginning to erode and fragment some of the patches of flowers in the valley bottom — a sad symptom of the pressure of tourism.

Primroses grow in woodland clearings, hedgebanks and fields up to the 1000-foot contour. Most people have childhood memories of these sweet-scented flowers. We recall the closing of Llanberis School in Minehead in 1945 when the elderly headmistress, Miss Benison, pince-nez aquiver, took her pupils by bus to Selworthy Lane to see the primroses on that last afternoon. Other springtime flowers in the woods are wild daffodils, green hellebore, yellow archangel, wood sorrel, wood anemone, bugle, early purple orchid, red currant, wood dog-violet and moschatel. The latter is a three-inch high yellowish plant, which was once used as a symbol of Christian watchfulness, on account of its five faces atop each stem looking north, south, east, west and heavenwards. Then we have goldilocks, a member of the buttercup family which never seems to have its fair share of petals. Bluebells, elsewhere a feature of beech woods, can be seen in equal glory in some of our oak woods, notably in the Brendon Hill, Dulverton and Porlock Parks areas. We will never forget the sight of bluebells growing in Helebridge Wood in the 1960s where they formed a carpet mixed with pink purslane, stitchwort and water avens. This site has since been spoilt by tree felling. Sometimes bluebells spring up and cover a hillside after removal of a wood, where there were apparently none before the trees were cut. The shade had been too dense for them to produce flowers until the sun's warmth was restored. However, with the trees gone and *all* shade removed they seldom last long in these situations. A similar phenomenon sometimes occurs with foxgloves.

Later in the year more lovely-named flowers come: sweet-woodruff, enchanter's nightshade, common avens (herb Bennet), Welsh poppy, common twayblade, broad-leaved helleborine, yellow pimpernel, cowwheat, sanicle, wood sage and golden rod, with more rarely, nettle-leaved bellflower. Occasionally, where there are beech leaves or stumps, the saprophytic bird's-nest orchid occurs. In the Lynmouth area Irish spurge, which apart from its native Ireland is only found here and in Cornwall, and toothwort parasitic on hazel are found.

Typical woodland grasses are creeping soft-grass, wood meadow-grass wood millet and melic. Remote sedge and wood sedge are frequent. The soft grass is usually called by botanists 'hairy knee'd Molly', this being an indentification aid as the knee-like joints of the stem are covered with a ring of hairs. Why Molly? — its botanical name is *Holcus mollis.*

Conifer Plantations

Most of the large conifer plantations of the Forestry Commission have grown since the 1920s. The most frequently planted conifers are European and Japanese larches, Norway and sitka spruce, lodgepole, Corsican, Monterey and Scots pines plus some Douglas firs and western hemlock. Monterey cypress and western red cedar are often planted for shelter belts. Present day uses of the timber are paper making, chipboard, pit props and building supplies. Few herbs will grow beneath conifers except along the forest rides, but the plantations provide habitat for fungi, lichens, certain insects, and they give cover for deer (mainly fallow) and birds such as siskin and crossbill. Piles of cones with their scales stripped by grey squirrels to extract the seeds are a familiar sight. The area of Scots pine on Culbone Hill was planted about 1870 and must have proved a commercial disaster, but the stunted, lichen clad trees hiding the mysterious Culbone Stone are an Exmoor feature. On National Trust land the trend nowadays is to mingle other trees with conifers, resulting in a more natural landscape.

Remnants of conifer plantations in the Barle Valley near Simonsbath.

Colin Thornton

Selworthy Woods

One large area of woodland has not yet been mentioned. This is Selworthy Wood which may prove a disappointment on a first visit as it contains much holm oak and cherry laurel — evergreens which are as sparse in ground flora as a conifer wood. We are, personally, rather fond of the oaks which have a most attractive bark, giving a reptilian prehistoric impression. They were planted with other species, thousands at a time from 1809 to 1826 by Sir Thomas Acland, 10th Baronet of Killerton and Holnicote, as a marker each time he had a child. He had nine children! At the top of the wood is a stone hut, with a seat in memory of the much loved Sir Thomas. Verses by Keble and Heber, oft quoted by Sir Thomas, appear on wall plaques, and their content gave rise to the local name for the building, 'wind and weather hut'. All this land is now National Trust owned.

Coastal Woods

There are nearly 1000 ha of coastal woods growing behind North Hill, Minehead, between Porlock and Lynmouth and at Woody Bay. At Culbone and Glenthorne they are remarkable in the way they slope right down to the very edge of the shingle beach. Trees, in this salt-laden, windy atmosphere grow less well than inland and are shallow rooted on the friable cliffs. Their weight, plus heavy rains, combined to cause a major landslip a few years ago which carried away much of the footpath from Porlock Weir to Culbone. These woods include some uncommon whitebeam species and an attractive flower, wood vetch, which has white petals delicately veined with mauve. Wood spurge, wild madder and spindle also favour coastal areas. Sycamore has increased in recent years and now covers some quite large areas.

Coastal Flowers

Rhododendron, that loved and hated shrub, is perhaps most spectacular where it blooms on coastal slopes in May. It would be nice if it could be allowed to flourish in one or two of these situations and be eradicated elsewhere where it is slowly advancing to the detriment of other wildlife. Yew is also a feature of the cliffs below Martinhoe where it grows, flattened to the contours by the wind.

Nature's rock-garden on the sea-cliffs is a most colourful sight, with cushions of thrift (remember the illustration on the old twelve-sided three penny bit?), kidney vetch, sea campion, thyme, rock stonecrop, sheep's-bit and rock samphire forming a pink, yellow, white, mauve, blue and green mosaic — the only problem being that you may have to hang over an 800-ft.-high ledge, or risk being cut off by the tide to appreciate them! Sea beet, scurvy grass, anise-scented fennel, houndstongue, ploughman's spikenard, storksbill and viper's bugloss can be seen near the strandline of the beaches with less risk to life and limb. The bugloss was used in the past as a cure for snake-bite—the nutlets being said to resemble a viper's head. Carline thistles occur on the Foreland, rock spurrey at Hurlstone, and silver ragwort is well established on the cliffs at Glenthorne. Yellow horned poppy, with the longest seed-pod of any British plant can also be found at the extremities of the National Park — near Combe Martin and Minehead.

Saltmarsh plants are sea spurries, sea aster, sea arrowgrass, sea purslane, seablite and glasswort. The latter two in the past were burned to produce carbonate of soda for use in glassmaking. Saltmarsh rush also covers quite a large area at Porlock Weir.

At Minehead the Exmoor Natural History Society manages a short 'wild flower walk' by courtesy of Somerwest World, where Greek dock, goat's rue, teasels and about one hundred other flowers may be seen in summer.

Hedgerows

We have jumped ahead. Before many of the coastal plants bloom, hedgerows come to life after the winter. Tiny leaves have been on the honeysuckle since Christmas and, for weeks, hazel catkins have looked on the verge of dropping open, just waiting for some sunshine before releasing their pollen on the breeze, to be caught downwind by the minute red bristles of the female flowers. The 'pussy willow' catkins are the male flowers of either goat or common sallow, the greenish female flowers are borne on separate trees.

On the higher moors the traditional hedging material is beech and few Exmoor views lack a beech hedge. The art of laying such a hedge is a craft to be proud of. The saplings, usually planted atop an earth and stone bank, are partially cut a few inches above the roots, bent over horizontally and woven together. The resulting growth is a weatherproof shelter for stock, and a source of beech logs and posts every few years when re-laying takes place. It is sad to see the modern way of dealing with hedges skilfully built up over the centuries by the 'hedgers'. Today a man sits enclosed in the cabin of his flailing machine, from which he rarely descends, and drives on, partially sighted and deafened, regardless of holes that need filling, likewise of nesting birds or patches of flowers which would have received care from the man on foot. The aftermath of splintered branches, torn nests and bruised plants is a form of progress we could do without on Exmoor.

However some farms do still hedge by hand, and subsidies are now available for this work.

Comparatively few plants grow in the upland hedgebanks but if we come down 500-600 feet into the sunken lanes, we find a different picture. A way of calculating the age of a mixed hedgerow is to count the number of *woody* plants in its make-up over a distance of 30 yards. Each species is said to represent about a hundred years — but you must discount any originally planted species. We and others have tested this method on a few hedgerows where the age is known and it does seem to work out about right. It is in these old hedges that about one third of Exmoor's wild flowers can be found (c300 species). In spring, lesser celandines, common dog violet, dog's mercury, primroses, early purple orchid, germander speedwell, cow parsley, coltsfoot, white deadnettle, Jack-in-the-hedge, shining cranesbill, navelwort or pennywort, wild strawberry and greater stitchwort (which we used to call 'Stars of Bethlehem'), occur — lovely names for enchanting flowers.

These are followed in season by various fumitories, a name meaning 'smoke-like'; and a drift of this plant scrambling up a hedgerow does have a smokey appearance; by roses of many varieties from white field rose to deep pink downy rose; red, white and bladder campions; herb Robert; rosebay and other willowherbs (particularly on the Brendons where the pink spikes adorn the roadsides for miles on end); clovers, vetches, hedge woundwort and yellow toadflax. Descriptions of all would overflow this book. Many of these plants, together with brambles, nettles and grasses are important food-plants for butterflies.

Common hedgerow shrubs include field maple which may grow into a charming small tree, blackthorn, willows, hawthorn, elder, holly, elm and, less frequently, spindle with its insignificant greenish flowers followed by waxy pink fruits which burst to release bright orange seeds. Its twigs were once used for meat skewers and, presumably, spindles. Dogwood with white flowers and black berries is most conspicuous in winter when its red twigs show up. Bullace or wild plum is occasional.

Honeysuckle climbs by twining, always in a clockwise direction, i.e. the sensitive tip of the shoot follows the movement of the sun. As it twines around the stems of other shrubs such as blackthorn, it often constricts their growth and these spirally marked shoots are frequently sought by walking-stick makers.

On the Holnicote Estate an uncommon hedging material has been used extensively. This is a species of barberry *(Berberis glaucocarpa)*. It makes a good thick spiny hedge when kept trimmed but in some places (other than Holnicote) it has been 'let go' so that it forms a thick over-grown shrubbery which bears rather attractive yellow flowers followed by blue-black berries. A tree which is scarce nationally occurs in hedgerows in the north-east section of Exmoor, particularly in the Avill and Porlock Vales. This is black poplar, the male trees being conspicuous by their long red catkins in spring. It is considered to be native but may have been introduced in ancient times as it had various medicinal properties, an ointment being made from the buds. 'Black' is a misnomer and was probably originally used just to differentiate it from the white poplar, which also occurs here.

Hedgerow fruits in autumn include elderberries and sloes eagerly sought by wine-makers, blackberries for tarts and jams, raspberries rarely with yellow fruits, and strawberries just to eat and enjoy — but **please** leave some for the birds and mice! Fortunately, spraying of hedgerows does not take place on Exmoor and the biggest threat to our hedgerow flora is the machine cutting — cutting too close and too early, before the flowers have seeded; but we are pleased to note recently the trend towards a happy compromise whereby the lower strip nearest the traffic is cut, leaving the higher sections to flower and seed. Sadly, hundreds of miles of hedgerows have been lost in recent years due to road widening and enlargement of fields which spell disaster not only to the plants, but also to the insect, mammal and bird life present.

Around the Villages

The flower filled lanes lead from one village or hamlet to another and as we approach habitations, the flora changes; partly because building materials contain alkaline substances encouraging the growth of plants which cannot tolerate Exmoor's mainly acid soils, and partly because the activities of man carry seeds both intentionally and unintentionally to his homeland. Nettles are always a sign of man either in the past or present and, in cultivated soil, many annual weeds grow (ask any gardener) which spread into nearby hedgerows. Primroses thin out through past picking and uprooting, but there are indications that — with the growing trend towards conservation and a few prosecutions — they are increasing again in these situations. It is now an offence to dig up wild plants without the consent of the landowner.

Dog's mercury, abundant in the wild, becomes scarcer in gardens where annual mercury may be found in its place. Wavy bittercress gives way to hairy bittercress and germander to slender speedwell. Red deadnettle, petty spurge, groundsel, ground elder and couch grass abound if your garden is like ours, also bindweed, locally called withywind. A blue variant of scarlet pimpernel occurs in one or two gardens. Sometimes, extra deep digging will release seeds which have lain dormant in the soil from times before the building of houses. Shepherd's needle and yellow star-thistle are examples from recent years. In 1976, the year of the drought, lawn cutting was superfluous and dozens of autumn ladies tresses, a tiny orchid with flowers spiralling up the stem, were reported. They were not really a freak of the hot weather, but had previously just been mown down!

Then there are garden plants which have escaped and are now accepted as part of our wild flora. Yellow corydalis and red spur valerian on walls are examples. Friends of the authors will by now be only too familiar with the story of the parson who had recently moved to West Somerset. He was somewhat alarmed one day when his gardener came to him with the query "Do 'ee want I to knock down them drunkards on your wall?" ('Drunkards' — local name for the valerian being likened to red noses). In 1985 the Exmoor Natural History Society conducted a survey of garden weeds, and from 31 gardens 302 different weeds were recorded with an average of 55 species per garden. Dandelion was the only plant found in every garden.

Another interesting survey was run in 1982 by the Botanical Society of the British Isles. This was an examination of parish churchyards. We did the Somerset section of Exmoor and its environs which involved visiting 40 churchyards. This proved of great value as 'God's acre' is often the only remaining piece of ancient grassland in a district. It sometimes retains relics of herbs planted in the past, when it was believed that their healing properties would be increased if grown in holy ground. Carhampton churchyard, at 100-foot altitude was the most prolific with 117 species, whereas Stoke Pero at 1025 feet had about 40. However, the highest, Simonsbath, had around 70 species because a large area was left uncut. Exford was particularly interesting with betony, Welsh poppy, ransoms, thyme-leaved sandwort and some rare ferns and liverworts. Wootton Courtenay was notable for ivy broomrape.

Perhaps some of the most interesting plants around villages are those brought in the past as potherbs, medicines or for dyeing. 'Officinalis' or 'Officinale' as the specific (2nd) part of a botanical name signifies that a plant was available from herbalists, e.g. *Taraxacum officinale* (Dandelion) — similar to today's list of drugs issued to medical practitioners.

Some of the more interesting plants you may see around Exmoor villages:—

ALEXANDERS —	'The parsley of Alexandria' grown as a potherb but needed blanching, like celery, to be really palatable.
MARJORAM —	A general 'cure-all' often taken as herb tea.
GREATER CELANDINE —	A yellow member of the poppy family once used to treat eye disorders. An unusual orange variety grows near Cutcombe. 'Celandine' derives from the Greek 'Chelidon' for swallow — it flowers at the time these birds return.
FEVERFEW —	Widely used in the treatment of fevers and headaches, has recently had a comeback for migraine sufferers.
SOAPWORT —	A soapy substance could be obtained from the leaves.
DANEWORT —	Very rare on Exmoor but present in two or three places. A plant surrounded in legend including one that it sprang from the blood of slain invading Danes. It *was* in England in Anglo-Saxon times but its old name was Walwort. The name Danewort seems to have been first used in 1538.
LADY'S MANTLE —	A plant noted for its pleated, mantle- or cloak-shaped leaves which catch dew drops — very important in magical potions hence its botanical name *Alchemilla* — a little plant used by alchemists. It had important healing properties and was widely used in treating many things from wounded battlemen to sick cows. The plant was so important that with the coming of Christianity it was given the name Our Lady's Mantle to counteract its former magical associations.
EVERGREEN ALKANET —	The 'little alcanna' a name derived from the Arabic al-henna ascribed to the henna plant used by Egyptian women as a red cosmetic dye. A red dye was produced also from Alkanet.
SWEET CICELY —	A pot-herb with a strong aniseed flavour and scent.
HOP —	Fairly widespread although it has never been cultivated on the scale of the hop fields in south-east England. Used in beer making.

Many plants have been used for centuries by children in their games: we have a charming book with coloured plates entitled *Plants We Play With,* issued at the turn of the century. This describes twenty children's games involving plants including 'Do you like butter?' (buttercups held under the chin), walnut shell boats, daisy chains, dandelion 'clocks', throwing sticky burrs, conkers, 'tinker, tailor . . .' with rye grass, and 'champions' similar to the game of conkers but played with ribwort plantain. Whistles were made from willow or elder twigs. All these we played in *our* young days and the only game in the book not applicable to Exmoor is 'cowslip balls' as this plant is very scarce here. Do present-day children still play these games, or look for the fairies' shoes hung inside white deadnettles, or for 'lords' (dark coloured spadex) and 'ladies' (light coloured) in wild arum, and supplement their diet with mallow 'cheeses' or new hawthorn leaves?

An introduced tree common on many village greens, e.g. Horner, and Bossington is the walnut; our forefathers made sure that they planted something useful as well as ornamental — perhaps local authorities could follow suit and give us chestnuts and plums in our streets!

Waterside Plants

Few Exmoor villages have a pond but most have a stream running through, providing yet another plant habitat. In the moorland springs where the streams rise, there is almost invariably water blinks with its bright green leaves and probably moorland crowfoot nearby. As the waters run through the combes and gradually increase in size, water milfoil hides lurking trout, and water mint scents the banks. Lower still, fool's watercress, hemlock water dropwort, angelica, codlins and cream (local name for Great willowherb — codlins is a type of apple) and water figwort add their colours. In many Exmoor waters the South American plants *Mimulus* have become established. There are various species: *Mimulus guttatus* or monkey-flower has mainly yellow blooms and is uncommon; *Mimulus luteus,* blood-drop-emlets with large red blotches is very rare but the hybrid between the two is the commonest form. The musk, *Mimulus moschatus,* has flowers only half the size, but the leaves and stems are covered with sticky hairs. It has not been recorded from Exmoor other than as an introduction, although it is known on the Quantocks and just south of the Exmoor border. This was the plant which used to be sold commercially for its sweet scent, until it suddenly became scentless about 70 years ago. Another garden plant which has spread spectacularly along some rivers, particularly the Barle, is *Montbretia.* Less welcome are the alien knotweeds; in places, e.g. Hunters Inn, they are increasing rapidly and smothering large areas. Butterbur favours stream banks and its huge leaves, which grow after the flowers fade, were once used for wrapping butter. Their umbrella-like size also led to their botanical name *Petasites* from the greek *Petasos* — a large hat.

Ponds and slow moving waters may have a green covering of common duckweed or water starwort, but you will need sharp eyes to spot the smallest British flowering plant, least duckweed — the whole plant is the size of a pin-head and if you can find its 'flower' — a minute stamen— you will make botanical history, for one has not so far been recorded in Britain. There are many types of pondweeds and recently, a grasslike plant, floating spike-rush, has been discovered, possibly spread by wildfowl. More spectacular are yellow iris and reedmace, the latter often mistakenly called bullrush. The true bullrush is much smaller. In brackish water in marshland dykes we find the three-petalled water plantain, celery leaved buttercup, sea clubrush and marsh woundwort.

Fields and Farms

Farming is an integral part of Exmoor and farmland supports a large number of plants not found much elsewhere. Meadow buttercups gild the lower fields in early summer and look lovely although they can be poisonous to cattle. The animals normally, however, have the sense to graze round them leaving little clumps all over the pasture. Ragwort is taboo in farmland but it does occur; the plants are only poisonous when dried. Hayfields have clovers and vetches and sometimes dog (or moon) daisies which used to be gathered and sold by gypsies. We will always remember seeing them growing freely on a gypsy's grave in an Exmoor churchyard. The main flowering period for dandelions is May when they can be as bright as any planted garden border.

In damp meadows we find cuckoo-flower, ragged robin, meadowsweet, kingcups and more rarely marsh valerian. Better drainage of farmland has diminished numbers in recent years, but the plants which have probably suffered most from modern farming are the cornfield weeds. Purified seed, spraying and ploughing as soon as the corn is gathered, have led to the decrease of many formerly common plants such as cornflower, corn cockle, weasel-snout, corn mint, field woundwort, field pansy, field forget-me-not, corn poppy, shepherd's needle, corn marigold and fluellen. Most of these can still be found in small amounts, except the first two. Common in field gateways is pineapple weed which releases its pungent fruity scent when trampled.

The Moorland

The last major habitat to describe is the moorland, most of which lies above the 1000-foot contour. This can be divided into three main types: Heather moors where *Calluna* is dominant; Grass moors, where grasses and sedges are dominant; and Heaths consisting of mixed species, mainly in the coastal and Brendon Hill areas. Broadly speaking, the grass moorland is in central Exmoor, much of which incorporates the old Royal Forest, surrounded by heather moors. Due to their altitude, it is late summer before the majority of moorland species come into flower, when for about a month there is a transformation of the usual sombre colouring.

Primroses occur in old woodlands or hedgerows.

David Doble

English Stonecrop grows on cliffs, walls and stony places near the coast.

Goatsbeard in fruit. The flowers which close by mid-day give rise to its other name of 'Jack-go-to-bed-at-noon'.

Mike Barbee

One of the first to flower is the bright bell heather, most abundant on the coastal heaths. About the same time the western gorse comes out and the two form a cerise and yellow patchwork, once seen not forgotten. The western gorse grows to about the same height as the heather and takes over for the short season when the taller common gorse is not in flower (giving rise to the saying 'when gorse is out of bloom, kissing's out of fashion'). In some seasons, particularly on North Hill at Minehead, many plants are covered with a red cobwebby parasite, lesser dodder. In time the red strands produce small pea-sized balls of pale pink flowers which belong to the bindweed family. Close examination will reveal where the roots grow into the host plant to draw their nourishment, re-lieving the dodder of the necessity of producing any leaves to manufac-ture its own food.

Less commonly, dodder can be found on whortleberry (bilberry) another very common plant. Although many people still gather 'worts' for putting into tarts and jam, I suspect that the traditional Somerset dish of junket and cream with whortleberries is rarely enjoyed these days. We met a man recently who said: "I like 'em freshly picked in a tart, and I al-ways freeze some and bring 'em out on Christmas Day." Nonetheless, in these affluent days, the 'wort-hills' are almost devoid of pickers. It is not so long since whole families would spend hot summer days on the hills picking the small fruits for sale. The tired labourers would be seen toiling home in July evenings laden with baskets, the sun-browned children stained purple — hands, faces, legs and clothes. In some local museums a device for whortleberry picking is displayed. This consists of a small scoop or trowel with a row of wire teeth along the front edge, and worked by combing the berries from the plants. Nicholas Culpepper (1616-1654) wrote of the 'whortle', "The ripe fruit is cooling, good to allay the heat of burning fevers; it is grateful to the stomach and creates an appetite."

Between the heather and whortleberry plants grow the small yellow flowers of tormentil, usually four- but sometimes five-petalled, heath milkwort which can have dark or light blue, cerise or white flowers, and heath bedstraw. Bristle bent-grass which soon turns a flaxen gold is com-mon on coastal heaths and wavy hair-grass is another pretty grass.

The central grass moors are the most desolate part of Exmoor. Damp areas like The Chains, where the annual rainfall averages 85 inches (Minehead = 34 inches) bear acres of purple moor-grass *(Molinia)* which changes from light bluish green when young, to darker, purple tinged mature leaves before turning yellow, and finally bleaching almost white in winter when it blows bleakly about in strands. There is also a vast area

63

of deer sedge on The Chains and tussocks of tufted hair-grass make walking difficult. In boggy places, the white 'cotton-wool' seed heads of cotton grasses bend in the wind. The taller harestail cotton grass has a single tuft, while the common cotton grass has several heads on each stalk. Sometimes an expanse of bog asphodel makes an unexpected splash of yellow. Its botanical name *ossifragum* means 'brittle bone' and refers to a disease which sheep were said to contract if they ate the plant, but the damp ground in which it grows was the true cause. Heath spotted orchids are sometimes seen in great quantity.

But surely the heather moors are the essence of Exmoor. Brown in autumn, black in winter, green in early summer and suddenly, in August, unbelievably pink when the flowers open. Beehives appear in places for the production of heather honey, and you can emerge from a walk across the moor with boots dusted thick in pollen. (At other times short heather is a fine shoe cleaner, brushing every trace of mud away). To keep the bushes young and healthy and to provide new green shoots for the hill sheep early in the year, the traditional management of a heather moor is swaling (burning). Care is needed to prevent the fire burning too fiercely and destroying the heather roots. Unfortunately, this has happened in some places, so that bracken has increased until it is now dominant on many hills.

The uplands are generally devoid of trees but brown birch, rowan, hawthorn and eared willow are common on combe sides where they provide food for birds in autumn. In two or three places the creeping willow, no higher than a heather bush, may be found.

For botanists, the combes and damper areas provide happy hunting grounds where hours may be spent seeking, and occasionally finding, rarities such as cranberry, crowberry, lesser and Irish butterwort, lesser and greater skullcap, or marsh speedwell. More easily found are lousewort and its big cousin red rattle, eyebrights, bog pimpernel, bog stitchwort, bog willowherb, creeping water forget-me-not, marsh violet, bogbean, bog St. John's-wort, ivy-leaved bellflower and the insectivorous round-leaved sundew. Marsh pennywort leaves are easily spotted but the tiny flowers take some finding. Former uses are reflected in some of these names — eyebright eye-lotion can still be obtained from herbal shops, but perhaps lousewort which was used to keep unwelcome visitors from the bed linen is in less demand nowadays!

A third heather found on Exmoor is cross-leaved heath or bog heather. Its leaves are arranged in fours up the stem, forming a cross, and the flowers are pale pink and bell-shaped. All three species of heather are occasionally found with white flowers. The bog plants are surely the cream of the Exmoor flora; a drainage ditch in the wrong place can, and frequently has, wiped out a whole community. It is vital to conserve the remaining areas.

Some Exmoor specialities

Some of the plants which grow commonly on Exmoor are eagerly sought by visiting botanists as they are scarce or absent in other parts of Britain, but there are a few other plants which are very rare both on Exmoor and nationally. Finding these always brings a thrill. Occasionally we have to wait years before the re-appearance of a plant. The Deptford Pink was recorded in 1960 from near Selworthy, but it was not until 1983 that one plant was found again only to be cut down by path trimmers next day (this notorious act even got a mention in the *Daily Telegraph*). That seemed like the end but in July 1988 one plant appeared again.

A very rare variety of white mullein grows on the Holnicote Estate. Nowhere else in Britain is it natural. Our variety has yellow instead of white flowers and is now under the watch of the National Trust. Opposite-leaved golden-saxifrage grows in almost every damp patch but the alternate-leaved one has only two known Exmoor sites. In favourable years lesser twayblade can be found, but it is difficult to spot this 3-inch high orchid which grows underneath heather and has a very short flowering period. Bastard balm has spectacular white and magenta flowers, but it is regularly cut down by hedgetrimmers where it grows beside the main road to Exeter. This plant, first found 'at Mr. Champernon's wood neere Totnes' in Devon in 1650 is still practically confined to south-west England.

Near the sea, sand catchfly — small insects adhere to its sticky calyx — Babington's leek, henbane, bee and green-winged orchids are sometimes seen. Broomrapes are curious plants, each species parasitic on some other plant. Greater broomrape is about two feet tall and grows on gorse or broom, other species attach themselves to ivy, composites or pea flowers. Occasionally, usually on agricultural land, the very poisonous thorn-apple appears. This has large white flower trumpets and spiny fruits the size of walnuts.

Just off the moor, near Molland, the Pyrenean lily has been known since 1889. Inevitably, it is known locally as the Molland lily; but I have never heard the Pyrenean valerian, which grows near Dulverton, alluded to as the 'Dulverton valerian'. Although profuse around Taunton, mistletoe is almost absent but there has long been a clump high on a false acacia tree at Timberscombe, and it occurs in some orchards where it was probably introduced.

Relative newcomers to Exmoor are New Zealand willowherb and Cornish moneywort, both low creeping plants with small pink flowers which may continue to spread. Exciting as these new finds are, perhaps the greatest thrill is when a plant, believed extinct, is re-discovered, possibly at a site where it was recorded in the last century. All botanists must be optimists at heart.

NON-FLOWERING PLANTS

All the plants so far discussed have been ones which produce flowers and seeds. We now come to the section of non-flowering plants which reproduce from spores.

Ferns

About thirty species of ferns grow within the National Park. The most prolific of course is bracken, frequently simply referred to as 'fern' e.g. a stag will 'lie-up in the fern'. It has a certain value providing cover for animals and creating a shade or mini-woodland type habitat for plants such as cow-wheat and bluebell, but its rate of spread in recent years, particularly into heather moorland, causes some concern. The reasons for its recent increase are not altogether clear, but over-burning of heather and the fact that is is no longer cut for animal bedding are no doubt contributory factors. Regular cutting is the best method of control, as spraying with 'Asulam' destroys any other fern species in the area.

To most people, ferns fall into one of two types: either the large frilly frond 1-2 foot in height, as found in woods and ditches or 'one of the little ones which grow on walls'. In the first category we have shield, bucklers and male ferns of various species, some, such as the hay-scented buckler-fern being quite scarce. There are also two varieties of lady-fern, one with a green midrib and the other purple. Rarities on Exmoor are limestone, beech and oak ferns. Parsley fern occurred on scree near Simonsbath but has not been seen since 1977. By streams in the higher combes is lemon-scented fern, and hard fern is widespread with its two distinctive fronds, one sterile and the taller one bearing the spores. In autumn the tips of the broad buckler-ferns are often seen to be twisted as if tied in a knot. This is actually a gall caused by a small fly which lays its eggs in the stem. As the larvae develop they burrow into the tissue causing it to coil up.

On walls and rocks we have spleenworts, rustyback, wall rue and bladder ferns. We are constantly on the look-out for forked spleenwort but none has been seen since the 1960s. Two very rare ferns are adders tongue and moonwort. Each have a characteristic spore-bearing spathe which grows up above the frond to a height of six inches or so. Moonwort was believed extinct on Exmoor but recently odd plants have been found and a colony of over one hundred was discovered in 1988. Filmy ferns are even smaller and rarer though both Wilson's and Tunbridge filmy ferns occur, but these exciting finds may be a disappointment to some as they can have the appearance of rather damp moss!

Harts tongue and polypody are familiar ferns, the latter often growing high up on old oaks. Sea spleenwort is found on coastal cliffs within reach of salt spray and water fern, a small duckweed-like plant floats on still fresh or brackish water. It is most noticeable after a frost when it turns bright red.

Horsetails and Clubmosses

The ancestors of both these groups were present in the ancient coal-forests and their fossilised remains are often seen in museums. Five species of horsetail are found of which wood horsetail is the rarest and great horsetail the most spectacular. This can grow to about three feet and has an ivory coloured stem supporting whorls of other thin green stems. Leaves are only vestigial and the plants consist almost entirely of stems which all fit together like the sections of a fishing rod. Fruiting stems of common horsetail often occur by roadsides where they may be mistaken for a tall, thin, pale brown fungus.

Clubmosses have dwindled considerably on Exmoor in the last century — three species have disappeared in the last fifty years — although they are still common in Snowdonia, northern England and Scotland. Perhaps this is just a natural fluctuation of their boundary as Exmoor is on the extreme edge of their distribution. A clubmoss is not a moss, but a higher form of plant which has developed water-carrying tubes (vascular bundles) similar to the veins in flowering plants. This enables them to grow much larger than mosses, in fact, the stagshorn clubmoss which remains in two known sites on the moor can reach over a yard in length. This plant creeps along under heather, its antler-like forked stems eventually producing a pale yellow stalk surmounted by a cone containing spores. Fir clubmoss has also been seen by us recently.

Mosses and Liverworts

Well over 300 species occur on Exmoor so only a very brief mention of one or two of the most familiar is possible. Mosses differ from (most) liverworts in having stems bearing leaves and fruit capsules which open by means of a 'lid'. Sphagnum mosses are very common in moorland bogs and their sponge-like qualities made them a valuable dressing for wounds; they were used extensively in wartime. The largest moss is common hair-moss and this is frequent in woodland. On areas which have been burnt, common cord-moss is often the first plant to re-colonise. White fork-moss forms cushions on woodland floors, sometimes breaking off and rolling about until it becomes a round, pale green, living 'tennis ball'. The feathery fronds of tamarisk feather-moss are most attractive and easily seen in shady places and, beside streams, the translucent leaves of *Hookeria* can sometimes be found. There are mosses which can be found growing on walls, tree trunks, banks, in heather or grassland — even indoors if you have pot plants.

Liverworts, so named from the liver-like creeping form of the larger species, are found on wet soil or tree trunks. *Pellia* is the commonest genus on Exmoor. In fruit this produces a round black knob at the end of a thin stalk (like a hat pin), the knob splits open in the form of a cross to release thousands of spores. Another genus *Marchantia* grows rarely on paths and its fruiting bodies are like miniature umbrellas. *Frullania* is a smaller type found on tree trunks where it sometimes gives a reddish tinge. The study of mosses and liverworts is a most interesting though specialised one.

Lichens

Lichens are quiet unique in the realm of plants for, instead of being a single plant, they are in fact a combination of two, partly fungi and partly algae. The fungus, lacking chlorophyll, unable to manufacture its own food, combines with an alga and the two grow together to produce a lichen — a quite amazing plant. They can grow almost anywhere, on bare rock, in Arctic regions or the desert, are undamaged by either sun or frost and therefore present all the the year round . . . but the one thing they cannot withstand is air pollution, and they are missing from most cities and industrial areas because of this. Their abundance on Exmoor, where there are probably around 400 species, is proof of a clean atmosphere. We must not be too complacent though, acid rain has recently caused their disappearance from the tops of some trees.

Lichens take one of three forms: crustose (forming a thin crust), foliose (with flat leaf-like sections) and fruticose (with short stems). Probably the fruticose group is the most noticeable for it includes the beard lichens *(Usnea spp.)* which often hang in festoons from old trees, sometimes almost covering them as on the stunted pines on Culbone Hill. One rare species *Usnea articulata,* an indicator of ancient woodland, is like a miniature string of sausages. We once found some used as lining in a raven's nest. Also in the fruticose group are *Cladonia* species, many typical on moorland. *Cladonia coccifera* has inch-high stems surmounted by scarlet blobs with the appearance of sealing wax. A similar plant *C. chlorophaea,* opens out at the top to form a miniature wine-glass shape or 'pixy-cup'. A third, *C. portentosa* (formerly *C. impexa)* resembles a small lump of wire wool and is very common on damp moorland.

In the foliose group we commonly find *Evernia prunastri* on trees. Its strap-shaped thallus is greyish above and white beneath. It is widely known as 'oak moss' (although it is a lichen) and has been used for many purposes including perfumery, dyeing, shotgun wadding, an antibiotic, and by long-tailed tits which combine it with cobweb to make their elastic sided nests. A species almost confined to mediaeval woods is tree lungwort *(Lobaria pulmonaria).* Now rare in most of Britain, it occurs in Horner, Hawkcombe and a few other sites. It was once sold as a cure for lung diseases and has also been used as a substitute for hops in beer-making. Large grey dog lichens often attract attention, particularly when the orange *apothecium,* (fruiting bodies) are present. Bright orange *Xanthoria* grows in a variety of habitats, including rooftops. A freshwater species, *Dermatocarpon fluviatile* is a rare lichen occurring on rocks in our upland streams. On coastal shingle another bright orange species, *Caloplaca marina,* is particularly conspicuous near Porlock and some coastal cliffs are thickly encrusted with Sea Ivory *(Ramalina siliquosa).*

A crustaceous lichen found below the high tide level is the black *Verrucaria mucosa.* Letter Lichens *(Graphis spp.)* are silver-grey crustose lichens common on smooth tree trunks, the fruiting bodies form black lines with a resemblance to writing. Map lichen *(Rhizocarpon)* is similar but grows on rocks or walls and is yellowish-green with black lines, not the fruiting body in this case but a sort of breathing space around the thallus which lacks any green algal cells. These lines resemble the outlines of counties or countries as they may appear on a map.

The full potential of lichens is a subject still under study and there is much more to be learned about their distribution, uses and taxonomy.

Fungi

Over 500 fungi are recorded in *The Flora and Fauna of Exmoor* and that is only the tip of the iceberg. There are slime moulds and flask fungi, earth tongues and cup fungi, rusts and smuts on plants and jelly fungi. Bracket fungi, such as Beefsteak on oak, Polypore on birch, and Dryad's saddle on elm are found, often high up on the trees, while on the ground are puffballs, stinkhorns, earth stars, and the half-inch diameter bird's-nest fungi, shaped like its name and containing tiny 'eggs', actually bags of spores which disperse as raindrops fall on them. Hard, round, charcoal-like King Alfred's Cakes are common on ash trees.

But none of these are what immediately spring to mind as typical fungi. Ninety-nine out of a hundred people probably first picture either an edible field mushroom sizzling with bacon or the (closely related) poisonous fly Agaric — red with white spots. There are many edible mushrooms besides the common one: chanterelle or giant puffball are delicious, but don't experiment unless certain of indentification — many are poisonous and some are deadly. Also, certain species can cause trouble if consumed with alcohol.

The cap fungi divide roughly into two groups, those which have gills, as the field mushroom, and those which have spongy pores visible under the cap. These pores are actually the open ends of tubes. Spores are held in either gills or tubes and the spore colour is an aid to the identification of many species. If a mushroom cap is left overnight on a piece of white paper, some spores will fall out making an interesting pattern and a spore-print can be obtained.

The *Russulaceae* are an attractive family of gill fungi, found in many colours: purple, milk-white, yellow, pink, red, brown and olive green; milk caps which exude a milky substance also belong to this family. The smaller wax caps are another colourful group. Death cap is uncommon but the false death cap occurs frequently. Shaggy ink-cap, also called lawyers wig, is well-known, and parasol mushroom, brown with white spots, you have probably eaten unknowingly in mushroom soup! Of course fairy rings, subject of much legend and speculation, are known from childhood. Generally, they are caused by a type of **Agaric**, *Marasmus oreades* which has a perennial mycelium which spreads outwards at the rate of between six to twelve inches annually. Thus the approximate age of a ring can be calculated. Cap fungi with pores are members of the family *Boletaceae;* one, found in woodlands, is known as 'currant bun' due to its brown, sticky cap.

Giant Puffball sometimes acquire football size and can weigh over 8lbs. Fairly common in grassland. Delicious!

Peter Davis

Many small species of fungi often go unobserved, but a search among fallen twigs, heather, grass or pine needles can expose exquisite little fungi. The dainty horsehair fungus has wiry hair-like stems; the nut cup grows on fallen hazel nuts, others grow on pine-cones or bramble twigs and the scarlet caterpillar fungus grows on dead insect larvae or pupae buried in the ground. Green oak which stains the wood used to make Tunbridge ware is common, but it is harder to find the fruiting cups, the colour of verdigris. Orange peel fungus and red elf-cups are more noticeable. Yellow brain fungus is very common on gorse and is one of the jelly type *(Tremella)*. We could write many pages on the fungi of Exmoor but as space does not permit, we will conclude with a true story.

One day at the Malmsmead Field Centre, we were approached by some wide-eyed holiday makers, camping in the adjoining field. Could we offer an explanation for a phenomenon they had experienced by their campfire the preceding evening? A pile of branches stacked ready for burning had begun to glow with a ghostly light. In daylight they appeared quite normal. We were able to confirm that this was nothing supernatural. *Very* close inspection of the broken ends of the logs showed the wood permeated by whitish strands — in fact the mycelium of Honey fungus. When damp and actively growing this can become luminous — in fact it caused several false alarms for fire-watchers at timber yards in the war.

Algae: Freshwater and Terrestrial

Everyone has seen algae but few know much about them. One of the commonest and simplest is *Pleurococcus,* the green film covering damp tree trunks, fences, etc. Each plant consists of a single microscopic cell, containing chlorophyll which enables it to produce its own food from the air, sunlight and moisture, i.e. photosynthesis. This differentiates a plant from an animal cell which cannot manufacture its own food. Both can reproduce by division of the cell. Algae are divided into various classes, the main ones being Blue-green, Green, Brown, Red and the diatoms. Not all are single celled however. Anyone with a garden pool will be too well aware of blanket weed, a filamentous alga, and in moorland pools we find strands of *Spirogyra* and *Ulothrix.* Others are found on damp earth.

Marine — (Seaweeds)

The marine algae, better known as seaweeds, can have a very different appearance. They also divide into colour groups: Brown, Green and Red. Some are a source of iodine. The largest are the kelps: furbelows is a brown weed up to two metres in height. It grows on the lower shore, just below low water-mark, but on spring tides the tops of the plants are exposed and one becomes aware of miniature marine forests. Despite their large size, they only live for one year and can produce no roots like a flowering plant. Instead, they are fastened to the sea bed by a warty suction pad or 'holdfast'. *Laminaria* species — sea belt and oarweed — grow similarly. On the middle shore we find bladder, egg and serrated wracks.

Laver falls within the largest, the red group of seaweeds. It is locally frequent and, although less than formerly, it is still gathered and may be purchased in jars from delicatessen shops. Fried with bacon it is the local delicacy known as 'Laver Bread'. Sea oak with fronds indented like oak leaves is often epiphytic, that is growing on stems of other weeds; carragheen is a perennial attached to stones and dulse occurs in similar situations.

The green group includes sea lettuce and *Enteromorpha* species. The tubular fronds of the latter thickly cover rocky shores, generally at the mouth of a stream. It also occurs in brackish waters such as in the ditches on Porlock Marsh, and is a food source for many of the molluscs.

★ ★ ★ ★ ★

Thus we come to the end of our descriptions. We have tried to give a brief outline of what we find on Exmoor and hope this will encourage others to go out and see for themselves the great variety of plants and creatures which surround us. There is endless enjoyment to be had from the study of God's creation.